THE BRITISH MUSEUM

Illustrated

ENCYCLOPAEDIA

of

Ancient Rome

Mike Corbishley

THE BRITISH MUSEUM PRESS

This libellus is dedicated to Isabel and Lily who, one day, should read Catullus, and to their grandmother, mother and father, who have stood patiently to be photographed among so many ancient Roman monuments.

© 2003 Mike Corbishley

Mike Corbishley has asserted the moral right to be identified as the author of this Work.

First published in 2003 by The British Museum Press
A division of The British Museum Company Ltd
46 Bloomsbury Street, London WC1B 3QQ

A catalogue record for this book is available
from the British Library

ISBN 0 7141 3021 4

Designed, edited and produced by
Hilton/Sadler
63 Greenham Road
London N10 1LN

Cover design by Ewing Paddock

Typeset in Novarese Book
Printed and bound in Spain by Grafos SA

THE BRITISH MUSEUM
Illustrated
ENCYCLOPAEDIA
of
Ancient Rome

Contents

How to use this book

Welcome to the *Illustrated Encyclopaedia of Ancient Rome*. The encyclopaedia contains entries arranged in alphabetical order, starting with **Actors** and finishing with **Zenobia**. You can look up information on the whole variety of ancient Roman life, including places, famous people, everyday life, religion and sport. For example, **Britain**, **Carthage and Hannibal**, **Stagecoaches**, **Centurions**, **Chariot racing**, **Shops** and **Clothes**.

Inside most entries you will see some words printed in **bold type**. Whenever you see this you know that the word has an encyclopaedia entry of its own, which you can then look up to find extra information.

If you are not sure where to start reading in the alphabetical entries, you can try following a Roman trail. These trails are explained in more detail on pages 6 and 7.

If you cannot find something you are looking for in the main part of the book, try looking in the index starting on page 156.

Maps

On the page opposite you will find two key maps showing the lands that the Romans gradually conquered.

A word about dates

You will see the letters BC and AD used with dates for important events in this encyclopaedia. The system of dates used by many countries today is based on what is believed to be the date of the birth of Christ. BC is an abbreviation for 'Before Christ'. The years BC are counted backwards – for example, the Roman emperor Julius Caesar invaded Britain in 55 BC and then again the following year, in 54 BC. The last year of this form of counting dates is 1 BC.

After that, the letters AD are put in front of the date. AD is an abbreviation for the Latin words *Anno Domini*, which mean 'In the year of the Lord (Christ)'. The dates AD are counted forwards. To see how this works, the Roman emperor Claudius invaded Britain in AD 43 while the Colosseum was completed thirty-seven years later in AD 80. For dates nearer our own time we usually leave out the letters AD. Look back at the page opposite the Contents page and, towards the top, you will see the date that this book was published.

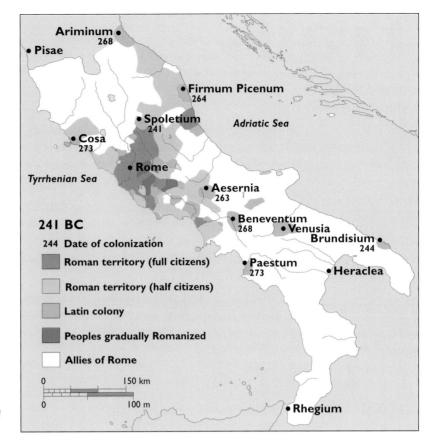

241 BC

244 **Date of colonization**

▨ **Roman territory (full citizens)**

▨ **Roman territory (half citizens)**

▨ **Latin colony**

▨ **Peoples gradually Romanized**

☐ **Allies of Rome**

0   150 km

0   100 m

*Right: This map shows the Roman territories during the 4th and 3rd centuries BC. During these centuries Rome controlled a number of territories. They forced the people they defeated to become allies of Rome or brought them into the state of Rome by making them citizens. 'Half citizens' had to pay taxes and, if necessary, fight in the army, but they did not have full rights as citizens. The Romans also established colonies (see **Cities and new towns**).*

Below: In this map you can see the extent of the provinces of the Roman empire by the beginning of the 2nd century AD. The Romans now controlled the whole of the Mediterranean area and parts of northwestern Europe.

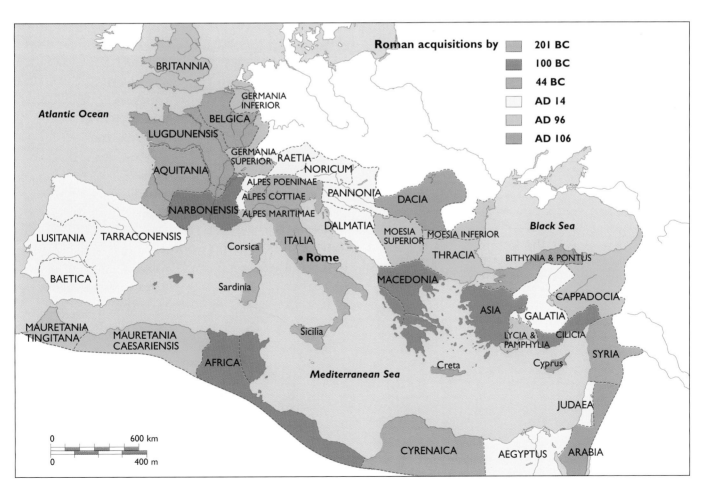

Roman acquisitions by

▨ **201 BC**
▨ **100 BC**
▨ **44 BC**
☐ **AD 14**
▨ **AD 96**
▨ **AD 106**

0   600 km

0   400 m

Trails

Follow a Roman trail
In order to help you find your way around this encyclopaedia, there are a number of 'trails' you can follow to discover related themes.

How to follow a trail
Look at the headings here and decide which topic you are most interested in. Let's say, for example, that you want to find out about the everyday life of ordinary Romans. All you have to do is look under 'Everyday Life' and you will find a list of entries from **Baths** to **Women**. The entries are in alphabetical order throughout the book, so you should not have any trouble finding the ones you want to read.

Every trail is identified by its own little icon, or symbol, so it's easy to spot them in the book. This icon is the one that will help you spot all the entries in the Everyday Life trail.

If you prefer, you can just browse through the book. Whenever you see this icon under a title, you know that the entry contains information on Everyday Life. You can follow all the trails in exactly the same way. You can also use the index starting on page 156 to find all the information you are looking for.

Happy hunting!

Trade & Transport

Amphorae
Cursus publicus
Import/export
Money
Ostia
Ports
Produce
Ships
Stagecoaches
Weights and
  measures

Crafts & Trades

Architecture
Bone working
Buildings
Glass
Jewellery
Metal working
Mosaics
Pottery
Sculpture
Wall painting

Conquering the World

Barbarians
Carthage and
  Hannibal
Eastern empire
Egypt
Empire
Etruscans
Gauls
Greeks
Provinces
Samnites
Settlements

Everyday Life

Baths
Children
Clothes
Doctors and
  medicine
Eating out
Family
Food
Meals
School
Shops
Slaves
Toys and games
Women

Country Life

Animals
Crops
Farming tools
Farms
Hunting and fishing
Olives and olive oil
Villas
Wine

City Life

Apartment blocks
Basilica
Cities and new towns
Colchester
Constantinople
Forum
Houses
London
Pompeii and
  Herculaneum
Rome

Engineering

Aqueducts
Bridges
Canals
Hypocaust
Lavatories and
  sewers
Machinery
Roads
Surveyors
Water supply

Warfare

Army
Auxiliaries
Cavalry
Centurions
Civil war
Cohorts
Forts
Hadrian's Wall
Invasion
Legions and
  legionaries
Masada
Navy
Sieges
Trajan's Column
Triumphs
Weapons and armour

Leisure & Sport

Actors
Amphitheatres
Chariot racing
Circus Maximus
Colosseum
Gladiators
Music
Playwrights
Theatres

Rulers & Officials

Augustus
Claudius
Constantine the Great
Consuls
Democracy
Dictator
Diocletian
Emperor
Equites
Hadrian
Julius Caesar
Justinian
Nero
Officials
Patricians
Plebeians
Pompey
Republic
Romulus and Remus
Senate
Tarquin the Proud
Trajan
Voting

Religion & Ceremonies

Burials and
  tombstones
Catacombs
Christianity
Foreign gods
Gods and goddesses
Household gods and
  shrines
Mithras
Priests and
  priestesses
Sacrifices
Statues
Temples
Weddings

Language & Writing

After the Romans
Calendar
Latin
Numbers
Writing

Actors

Actors were not thought to be respectable people in ancient Rome. They were often **slaves** or freed slaves. From **Julius Caesar**'s time, amateur actors performed on the stage, sometimes forced to do so by the **emperors**. Some actors became very popular with audiences and earned a fortune.

Roman actors needed skill to put on a performance and to cope with the huge audiences – the **theatre** of Marcellus in Rome, for example, held about 14,000 people. The **playwright** Terence tells us in his play *The Mother-in-Law* that actors had a lot to put up with when they gave a performance in the theatre. He talks of the audience being distracted by famous boxers and tightrope walkers and of the audience shouting and shrieking. We also know that actors sometimes shouted back at the audience. Only men were allowed to act in plays, and so they even had to play the female roles. By the 1st century BC, however, when mime and pantomime were introduced, **women** were allowed on the stage.

Actors wore special masks and costumes to help the audience identify which particular character they were playing.

This figurine of an actor is wearing a comic mask.

This carving shows the type of mask used in tragedies, which were serious plays. As well as identifying the characters in a play, masks may also have helped actors project their voices in the vast theatres so that members of the audience at the back could hear what was being said on the stage.

Aeneas

The Romans looked back to the **myths** of **Greece** for the origins of their own state. After the **Greeks** had beaten the Trojans in a great war, a famous Trojan leader called Aeneas left Troy for Italy, taking with him his father, Anchises, and his son, Ascanius. But Aeneas was no ordinary man.

His father was a Trojan king and his mother was the **goddess** Aphrodite (called **Venus** by the Romans). Aeneas also took with him the images of the **household gods**, and these were kept in the **temple** of **Vesta** in **Rome**. The poet **Virgil** wrote about Aeneas's epic journey in the *Aeneid*. Aeneas' son, Ascanius, whose clan name was Iulia, founded the town of Alab Longa near Rome, and **Julius Caesar** claimed he was descended from him. Caesar therefore claimed he was descended from the **gods** – the goddess Aphrodite, Ascanius's grandmother.

Africa

The Romans began to rule the **province** of Africa in 146 BC after they had defeated **Carthage**. In the beginning the province consisted only of what we know today as Tunisia, but the Romans made further conquests and new towns and

This fragment of a wall painting depicts the River Nile when Egypt, which is in northern Africa, was a Roman province. Notice the crocodile lurking at the bottom of the painting.

colonies were established (see **Cities and new towns**). The Roman province was extended from Libya in the east to Morocco in the west, with the mountain ranges and deserts forming the southern boundary, and the separate province of Egypt to the north. Africa supplied two-thirds of **Rome**'s corn. **Olives and olive oil** were exported, and the province was well known as the source of wild **animals** for the **amphitheatres** of Rome and elsewhere.

In addition to the letters AD (see page 4), you can see that the time and date on this building are given in Roman numbers – MCMXXIV. Turn to page 99 to work out when this clock tower was built.

Turn to page 99 to work out when this clock tower was built.

'The wild animal hunts, two every day for five days, are magnificent – I wouldn't deny it. But what pleasure can it give a person of taste when either a feeble human is torn to pieces by an incredibly strong wild animal or a handsome beast is transfixed by a spear?'
Cicero

After the Romans

V

One of the interesting things about the Romans is how much of their culture can still be found in our modern world. The remains of their **cities**, **forts** and **roads** can be seen throughout Europe. Many of our place names come from the Roman language, which was **Latin**. **London** is from *Londinium*, for example. Cities with the ending '-chester', such as **Colchester** and Manchester, were originally Roman forts (from the Latin *castra*, meaning 'camp'). The English language is full of Latin words, for example: *actor* – actor; *familia* – family; and *secundus* – second. Latin also influenced other European languages, such as French, Spanish and Italian. Scientists use Latin names for plants, animals and insects. And the **calendar** we use today is based on a Roman one.

Alexandria

The capital and main **port** of the **province** of **Egypt** was called Alexandria. It had been named after a **Greek** king, Alexander the Great, who established the city after conquering Egypt. It was famous for its gigantic **lighthouse**, which was one of the Seven Wonders of the Ancient World. In Roman times Alexandria was the port that sent vast quantities of corn to **Rome** to feed the city's poor.

Amphitheatres

Large numbers of Romans throughout the **empire** enjoyed a day out at the amphitheatre watching people and **animals** killing each other. Professional fighters, called **gladiators**, provided this gruesome entertainment. But there were also wild animal hunts, executions and prisoners fighting each other to death as a punishment. A special building was needed for these 'games', as they were called. The buildings were oval-shaped structures with many tiers of seats to allow as many people as possible to watch the 'entertainment' on the sand-covered floor, which was called the arena (the **Latin** word *harena* means 'sand'). The sand was there mainly to soak up the blood. A high wall around the arena stopped prisoners escaping and animals from leaping into the spectators. The animals could be raised to the surface in cages stored underground. The **Colosseum** in **Rome** had machinery for this.

Amphitheatres could also be flooded to allow sea-battles to take place to entertain the spectators. Sometimes there were even crocodiles in the water to eat anybody who fell overboard.

Left: The arena of the amphitheatre in Italica in Roman Spain, showing the underground area where the wild animals were kept. The floor above, where the battles and fighting took place, is now gone.

Below: The outside walls of the amphitheatre in Nîmes in Provence, southern France, are still in extremely good condition.

Amphorae

These are particularly large **pottery** containers that were used to transport and store liquids such as **wine**, oil and the fish sauce known as *liquamen*. Some are round-bottomed vessels, but many have pointed bottoms so that they could be easily stored in layers in the holds of **ships**. They have been found in **shops** at **Pompeii** pressed into the soft sand or earth floors of the storerooms. Sometimes the makers stamped on them their individual marks, or merchants wrote details of the contents they contained and the voyage.

Animals

Farmers bred a number of different animals and used them in more ways than most people do today. Most of them were for **food** – cattle, sheep, goats, pigs, chickens, geese and pigeons (as well as hares and snails), for example. But oxen, horses and donkeys were used for ploughing, riding and pulling carts and coaches (see **Stagecoaches**). Horses

'Cheese should be made of pure milk which is as fresh as possible. Some people mix in crushed green pine-kernels and curdle it, but you can make different flavoured cheese by adding any seasoning you like.'
Columella

The Romans used these iron 'sandals' to protect horses' feet. They were not nailed on to the hoof, like a modern horseshoe, but tied on to the leg. On the sole of the 'sandal' was a 'tread' to give the animal a grip on slippery surfaces.

were used by the **army** for pulling carts and for the **cavalry**. Commanders sometimes used other animals to attack or frighten the enemy – **Claudius**, for example, led the **invasion** of **Britain** with war elephants. The wool of sheep was used for cloth, and the skins of different animals were turned into leather for clothes and **shoes**. Animal horns and bone were carved into everyday objects and **jewellery** (see **Bone working**). Some cattle and goats provided milk, which could be used to make milk products such as cheese. Dogs were kept for hunting, to guard **houses** and **farms**, and to herd and protect farm animals. They were also kept

This Roman mosaic shows a domestic chicken. Most chickens were kept for their eggs and for their meat but we know that the Romans also bred the male birds for cock-fighting. These fights were very popular and people liked to place bets on the outcome of the contests.

as **pets**. Animal bones are often found on archaeological excavations and provide evidence for what people ate. We know, for example, that soldiers stationed on **Hadrian's Wall** in Britain ate quite of lot of mutton (the meat of old sheep) because large quantities of sheep bone have been excavated at some of the **forts** there. Animals were also killed as **sacrifices** to the **gods**, and wild animals were used to fight in the arena of **amphitheatres**.

These apartment blocks are in Ostia, a port not far from Rome. The steps you can see on the left, below a doorway, led to a staircase to the upper floors.

Apartment blocks

While some wealthy people could afford to live in **houses** with their families and had **slaves** to work for them, most people living in a city such as **Rome** had to make do with an apartment. These were built in blocks called *insulae*, the **Latin** word for islands, and could be just two storeys tall, perhaps converted from houses. Others were much higher, although the emperor **Augustus** allowed apartment blocks to be no higher than 18 m (60 ft).

Owners often ignored this law, however, and they were usually very bad about repairing and maintaining their buildings. Several writers of the time recorded their complaints about the quality of these buildings, as well as the lack of facilities such as water and **lavatories**.

It was not unusual for apartment blocks to catch fire or simply to collapse. These dangerous structures were the homes for very large numbers of people. We know that in Rome, in the mid-4th century AD, there were nearly 47,000 of these *insulae*.

The ruins of the Temple of
Aphrodite in Aphrodisias.

Aphrodisias

Aphrodisias, the city of the **Greek
goddess** Aphrodite (who was known
in Roman times as **Venus**), was in the
Roman **province** of **Asia** (modern
Turkey). Aphrodisias was a popular
visiting place for the generals **Sulla**
and **Julius Caesar** as well as for the
emperors **Augustus** and **Hadrian**. The
emperor Hadrian built a magnificent
temple for the goddess Venus. Like
many other temples, this one was later
converted into a **Christian** church.

In addition to this temple the city
had other fine **buildings** to recommend
it, including a **theatre**, which could be
converted into an **amphitheatre** for
gladiatorial shows (see **Gladiators**),
a stadium for athletics and **chariot
racing** and a very large public **baths**,
which was built by the emperor Hadrian.

Aphrodisias was well known for its
fine-quality marble and for its artists,
especially stone carvers, who travelled to
other provinces and to **Rome**.

*Stuff dormice [small
rodents] with minced
pork and also whole
dormice which have
been pounded with
pepper, pine-kernels,
asafoetida [a spice]
and liquamen [a fish
sauce]. Sew up the
dormice and put them
on a tile in the oven.*

*Stuffed dates: stone
the dates and stuff
with nuts, pine kernels
or ground pepper.
Roll them in salt and
fry in warmed honey,
then serve.*
Apicius

Apicius

One of the earliest cookery books that
has survived from ancient times was
written in **Latin**. Its author was given as
Apicius, but the recipes in *About Cooking*,
two of which are shown on the left, were

*A marble statue of the god Apollo, from Rome. At his feet are the
damaged parts of a mythical flying creature, the griffin.*

The emperor Valens built this magnificent aqueduct in Constantinople (now Istanbul) during his reign, AD 364–378.

probably compiled in the 4th or 5th century AD, long after Apicius's death (see **Food**).

Apollo

The **Greek god** Apollo was introduced into Roman worship (as the son of **Jupiter** and twin of **Diana**) through the **Etruscans** and the Greek **settlements** established in southern Italy. For the Greeks, Apollo was the god of music, medicine and prophecy. For the Romans, however, he was mainly the god of healing. The emperor **Augustus** was especially devoted to Apollo and built him a magnificent **temple** in **Rome**.

Aqueducts

An aqueduct (the word means 'bringer of water' in **Latin**) was usually just a water channel cut across country from a good source, such as a river or spring, to a town or city. Sometimes these were simply earth channels, while others were lined with stone. Some had to go underground in arched tunnels or be carried across rivers or valleys on high stone arches. One of the most famous of these is the aqueduct at Pont du Gard, which was built in the time of the emperor **Augustus** to carry water to the town of **Nîmes** in **Gaul** from a source 50 km (30 miles) away. **Rome** had eleven aqueducts that supplied it with water.

The best preserved aqueduct of the Roman world is at Pont du Gard, which is near Nîmes in southern France (known as Gaul in Roman times).

This gold ring was found in the town of Corbridge on Hadrian's Wall in Britain. It has an inscription in Greek, a language widely spoken in the eastern parts of the empire.

This modern re-enactment shows how Roman legionaries would have formed the siege tactic known as the testudo, using their shields linked together to protect themselves from enemy spears and missiles.

Arabia

The emperor **Augustus** mounted an expedition in Arabia, but it was not until the emperor **Trajan** that it came under Roman control in AD 106. Trajan made it a **province** to protect the trading caravans on their way from the east to **Syria**. Merchants from India brought spices, incense, gold and precious stones, and beyond that silk from China via the Red Sea. Trajan built a highway from Aqaba on the Red Sea to Damascus to help to protect this important trade route.

Architecture

From the late 1st century BC Roman architects could refer to a book written by **Vitruvius**, an engineer and architect. Architects worked for the state, the **emperor** and town councils to devise schemes for public buildings and works – from planning new towns to designing water and sewage systems (see **Cities and new towns**). The arch, vault and concrete were all important in Roman building.

Army

The Romans needed a large army to conquer and control all their territories. At first under the **republic** Roman soldiers were part-time. The two **consuls** called together all Roman citizens aged between seventeen and forty-six who owned property. They were assembled on the Capitoline Hill in **Rome**. The consuls had already appointed tribunes (staff officers) and they chose men for the various military units.

As Rome fought more and more wars, it needed a permanent army. Men volunteered to enlist, and be paid, in the army and navy. Soldiers, who were called legionaries, were organized into large units called legions (see **Legions and legionaries**). Each legion was commanded

'Titus Flavius Valens ... assigned to papyrus manufacture; Titus Celer – assigned to the river patrol boat; Titus Saturnius – to harbour dredging; Marcus Papirius Rufus – assigned to the granary in the Neapolis district of Alexandria as a secretary.'
From the army archives in Egypt in about AD 80

by a senior officer called a *legatus*. Normally there were 4,200 soldiers in a legion, but this number could be increased to about 5,000. By the 1st century AD there were about 5,500 men in a legion, including approximately 120 horsemen who acted as scouts and messengers (see **Auxiliaries**).

Each legion was organized into ten **cohorts** and then into smaller groups, called 'centuries', composed of about eighty men. Centuries were commanded by an officer called a **centurion**.

The army was not used just to conquer new lands. The huge Roman **empire** also needed to be defended against attacks from beyond its boundaries. Soldiers were also used to guard important places, such as quarries and mines, and act as customs officers at frontier points. Each legion had specialists, such as doctors, clerks and veterinary surgeons.

The consuls had their own bodyguards. These soldiers formed a Praetorian Guard. The emperor **Augustus** increased this guard to about 4,500 men to protect himself.

Asia

The Roman **province** of Asia (now Turkey) also included the island of Cyprus. The Romans called it by the name Asia Minor. Parts of it first came under Roman control when King Attalus III of Pegamum left it to Rome in 133 BC. **Rome** conquered the rest and established many towns. Asia was rich in natural products and manufactured goods – for example, woollen cloth, **wine**, fruit and marble – which were exported. Three of its main towns, **Aphrodisias**, Pergamum and **Ephesus**, had splendid buildings and large populations.

Cyprus was made Roman in 58 BC but had been part of Egyptian territory for nearly 250 years before that.

One of the main streets, lined with a colonnade, in the city of Pergamum, which is now in Western Turkey.

'The people of Claudiopolis are constructing a large public bath. Will you please send an architect at once to inspect not only the theatre but the bath as well.'
Pliny the Younger, as governor of Bithynia (now part of Turkey), to the emperor Trajan

The commemorative arch that was built by the emperor Hadrian now stands in a street in modern Athens.

war that followed, Octavian and **Mark Antony** ruled the Roman world between them. Mark Antony was based in **Alexandria** in **Egypt** while Octavian remained in Rome. Neither Octavian nor the **senate** would allow the Roman state to be split, so war was declared against Antony and **Cleopatra**, queen of Egypt, in 31 BC. Octavian won the war and declared peace for the Romans in 29 BC.

Octavian was now the most powerful man in the Roman state and in 27 BC he was given the title Augustus ('a person to be respected') by the senate. He became the first **emperor**. The eighth month of the year, Sextilis, was renamed Augustus – our August. Augustus secured the frontiers of the empire, and the **provinces** were controlled either by the senate or by Augustus himself.

Athens

Much of the ancient **Greek** city of Athens was destroyed by the **armies** of the general **Sulla** in the 1st century BC. Several Roman **emperors** later rebuilt or added to it. **Julius Caesar** and **Augustus** both put up public buildings. The emperor **Hadrian** spent three winters here and, after completing a huge **temple**, an **aqueduct**, a **gymnasium**, a library and a **bridge**, he erected a triumphal arch (see **Triumphs**) with an inscription on each side. One side read 'This is Athens, the ancient city of Theseus', but the inscription on the other side says 'This is the city of Hadrian and not of Theseus'.

Augustus

Octavian (later to be known as Augustus) was **Julius Caesar**'s adopted son and heir. In 44 BC, when Caesar was murdered, Octavian hurried back to **Rome** to avenge his death. After several battles in the **civil**

Bronze head of a statue of the emperor Augustus.

'Augustus was extremely handsome even when he was old but cared nothing for the way he looked. For example, he cared so little about his hair that, to save time, he would have two or three barbers working at the same time. While they were cutting his hair or giving him a shave he would be reading or writing something.'
Suetonius

A cameo carved portrait of the emperor Augustus. The jewelled headband is not original and was added in medieval times.

Augustus paid for the building or rebuilding of a number of public works, such as **aqueducts**, as well as religious buildings, such as **temples**, in Rome. The writer **Suetonius** tells us that he boasted: 'I found Rome built of sun-dried bricks. I leave her covered in marble.' Augustus died in AD 14 and had brought thirty years of peace to the Romans.

Auxiliaries

While legionary soldiers (see **Legions and legionaries**) were Roman citizens, auxiliaries were not. Auxiliaries formed the **cavalry** and light infantry units of the **army**. Auxiliary soldiers were often recruited because they had some special skills – they may, for example, have been archers or sling-shot throwers.

Auxiliary infantry soldiers were formed into groups called **cohorts**, each commanded by a *praefectus* – a prefect. As in the main army the cohorts were divided into 'centuries' commanded by **centurions**. On discharge, after twenty-five years of service, auxiliary soldiers received a grant of Roman citizenship.

B

Ballista

The Roman **army** used two similar artillery machines for **siege** warfare – the ballista and the catapulta. They were both made of wood and looked like huge crossbows on stands. They were very accurate and their twisted rope 'springs' fired stones (from the ballista) or iron-tipped bolts (from the catapulta) with enormous force.

Barbarians

'We have planted our crops only for an enemy to burn. All our resources are gone – the flocks of sheep, the herds of camels and horses. I am writing this behind walls, under siege.'
Synesius, a Christian bishop in the city of Cyrenaica in north Africa in the early 5th century

The Romans took the word *barbari* from the **Greeks**, who used it to mean anyone who was not civilized enough to speak Greek. The Romans used it for all those who lived beyond their borders and out of the reach of Roman civilization. In later Roman times it was the western **empire** rather than the **eastern empire** that suffered most at the hands of the barbarians. Visigoths (see **Goths**) from western Russia crossed the Danube in AD 376, Vandals from Hungary and Visigoths began to invade Europe in AD 409, and the Vandals took over north **Africa** in AD 429. German armies invaded Italy and their leader Odovacar declared himself king in **Rome** in AD 476. In another part of the Roman world, Saxons began to invade **Britain** in the 5th century AD.

Tombstones of cavalrymen often show them riding over and attacking one of their barbarian enemies. This is the tombstone of a cavalryman who served, and died, in Britain. His name was Rufus Sita and he came originally from Thracia (see the map at the bottom of page 5), which is now modern Bulgaria. The tombstone tells us that Rufus was forty years old when he died after serving for twenty-two years in the army.

Barracks

In permanent **forts** long, narrow, wooden or stone barracks were built for soldiers. Each barrack housed one century – usually ten spaces for the eighty men. The **centurion** in charge of the unit had his own room. The men stored their **weapons and armour** in a small front room and slept on bunks in the back. The soldiers ate in their barracks as there were no communal dining rooms.

These reconstructed barracks are at the Roman fort at Saalburg, near Frankfurt in Germany.

An artist's impression of the basilica attached to the baths at the town of Wroxeter in Roman Britain.

Basilica

A Roman basilica was a large, long, rectangular hall containing rows of columns that formed colonnades on each side of the interior. They were probably the largest buildings ever seen by some of the peoples the Romans conquered. A basilica was finely built with decoration inside, which usually included carved columns, **mosaic** floors and **wall paintings**. Light was brought into these great halls by rows of windows near the roof, as you can see above in an artist's impression of what a basilica looked like.

There was at least one basilica in every Roman town (see **Cities and new towns**), usually in the **forum**. They were used for great public or political meetings and for holding law courts. People might conduct their business here, or just meet friends. Large public **baths** also had a basilica that could be used as an indoor exercise hall, as the illustration above shows.

The term basilica was later applied to Roman **Christian** churches, which used the same design, and they were often reused in Roman times as churches. Cathedrals you can visit today are usually constructed in the style of a basilica.

People going to the public baths often carried with them their own supply of oil and scrapers (the strigilis). This set could easily be carried or slung from a belt.

Baths

Public baths were considered an essential part of Roman life, and there was at least one large bath-house in every city and town across the **empire**. **Pompeii** had three big baths for the public to use and by the 4th century AD there were nearly 1,000 in **Rome** itself (see **Cities and new towns**).

Public baths were not just for getting clean. They became places to relax, meet friends and conduct business. Some people used the baths like health clubs today. They swam and exercised and had massages. Baths were cheap to get into and children went free. Sometimes a rich person would try to win favour (or votes) with the townspeople by paying the baths to let people in free on particular days or weeks. Many people went to the baths once a day – the afternoon was the most popular time. Someone in a bath-

house in Pompeii had scribbled on the wall 'Jarinus you live here'. Some baths, such as the Stabian Baths in Pompeii, had separate facilities for men and **women**. If not, there were special times set aside for each sex – the mornings were usually reserved for women.

Going through the baths was a complicated affair. First, you undressed and left your clothes in a locker or on a shelf in the *apodyterium*. Then you passed into an unheated room called the *frigidarium* and probably had a dip in the

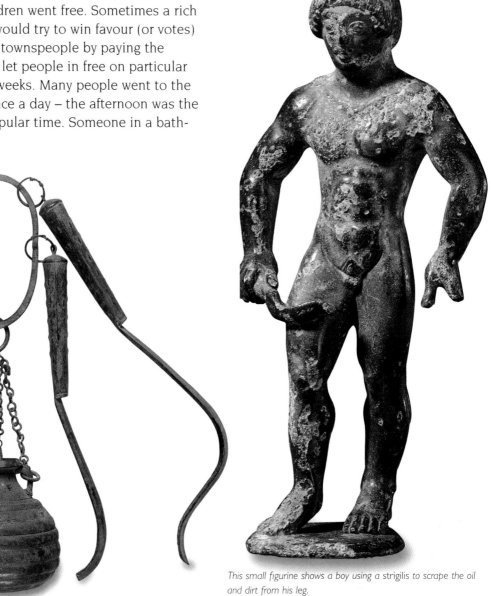

This small figurine shows a boy using a strigilis to scrape the oil and dirt from his leg.

cold pool. From there you went into a warmly heated room, the *tepidarium*. Your body was gradually getting accustomed to the heat. Next was the really hot room, the *caldarium*, which was like a Turkish bath today. It was full of steam (water was splashed on to heated pebbles), and there was a hot pool to bathe in and perhaps a warm fountain or basins to wash in. To get clean you rubbed yourself with **olive oil** or scented oils (or had your **slave** or the slave attendants do it). The steam opened your pores and the dirt was scraped off with a curved bronze instrument called a *strigilis*. Baths often had other facilities, too, such as a dry heat room called a *laconicum*, which was like a sauna.

After all this heat and sweat you would go back into the warm, and then the cold room to close your pores and perhaps have a swim in the pool and exercise in the open courtyard, the *palaestra*. Here you could chat with friends, have a game of dice, eat a snack or take part in some energetic exercise.

A large staff of slaves was needed to keep the baths going. Apart from cleaning, serving snacks, providing massages and plucking hair from the armpits of the bathers, they also kept the baths heated. The furnaces needed constant attendance in order to keep the **hypocausts** going.

Some wealthy Romans had smaller versions of the public baths in their own houses, especially at **villas** in the country.

Battering ram

The battering ram for breaking into walls or gates was made from an entire tree, which had a metal end often shaped to look like a ram's head. It was slung on an enormous wooden frame by ropes so that it could be swung by soldiers. The frame had wheels and was covered with leather hides or metal plates. The battering ram was often built into **siege** towers.

Bone working

Bones from **animals** were used to make all sorts of objects in the Roman world – hairpins, bracelets and rings as **jewellery**; combs, spoons and knife handles for the kitchen and dining room; dice and counters for games. Hinges for wooden boxes were also often made from long, round, carved tubes of bone. Different types of bone suited particular objects – the flat sections of the shoulder blades of sheep, for example, were ideal for cutting into the circular counters for board games (see **Toys and games**).

Above: Bone was an easy material to carve. These are examples of bone counters used for board games.

Right: Many hairstyles for women were very elaborate and involved using hairpins, such as this one made of bone. These pins were often carved with women's heads wearing the fashionable hairstyle of the day.

Bridges

At first the Romans built wooden bridges over rivers. The earliest recorded bridge was the Pons (bridge) Sulpicius, which was built to span the River Tiber in **Rome** in the 6th century BC. It is famous because it was this wooden bridge that Horatius and his two companions held against the invading **Etruscans**. A wooden bridge built by **Julius Caesar** across the River Rhine in **Germany** shows how good the Romans were at overcoming problems by clever engineering and construction.

Caesar was campaigning in Germany in 55 BC and needed to cross the Rhine, probably at Coblenz where the river is up to 500 m (1,600 ft) wide and 8 m (26 ft) deep. Wooden piles were driven into the river bed from floating platforms and beams fixed across them to form trestles. Then beams were fixed at right angles and wooden decking laid. The whole job took only ten days. The emperor **Trajan**, in his campaign against the Dacians, built a bridge across the Danube 1,500 m (nearly 1 mile) long, supported on stone piers 50 m (165 ft) high and 20 m (65 ft) wide.

Throughout the **empire** and in **cities** built on the banks of rivers the Romans built hundreds of stone bridges. Many survive today and some are still in use by modern traffic, as at **Trier**. The same techniques of building arches and spanning rivers were also used to construct **aqueducts**.

Britain

The land of Britain was on the furthermost edge of the Roman **empire** but was known to the Romans through trade with **Gaul**. **Julius Caesar** wrote about the wealth of metals there, and the geographer **Strabo** noted other possible exports: leather, hunting dogs and a supply of **slaves**. Britain was invaded three times by the Romans. Julius Caesar led two **invasion** forces in 55 and 54 BC but did not leave any troops there. The emperor **Claudius** led his own army from the south coast of Britain to **Colchester** in AD 43. This was the beginning of the conquest and occupation of Britain. It became the **province** of Britannia. Apart from some mountainous areas of Wales and northern Scotland, the rest of this remote island

'The population is very large, and there are very many farmhouses similar to those the Gauls build. There are a large number of cattle. For coins they use bronze or gold or iron bars. Tin is found inland, and small quantities of iron near the coast. There is also timber of every kind. All the Britons ... wear their hair long, and the men have moustaches.'
Julius Caesar writing about Britain

Left: A coin minted by the emperor Claudius celebrating his invasion of Britain. It shows an arch signifying his triumph 'over the Britons' (DE BRITANNIS). On the arch Claudius rides with piles of captured weapons.

Below: One of the bridges that crossed the River Tiber in Rome. It was built in 62 BC by Lucius Fabricius, the official in charge of road building.

became Romanized. In the 4th century AD troops were gradually withdrawn to cope with crisis after crisis nearer to home in Rome. In AD 410 the emperor Honorius sent a letter to the towns in Britain telling them that 'they must see to their own defences'.

Brutus

Marcus Brutus was a soldier who supported **Pompey** in the **civil war** against **Julius Caesar**. He plotted against Caesar with Cassius and they stabbed Caesar to death.

Buildings

The Romans, like us, built huge numbers of different types of building. This is the official catalogue of the buildings in one of the fourteen districts of **Rome** in the mid-4th century AD: 'City of Rome District III called Isis and Serapis contains ... a coin mint; the **Colosseum amphitheatre**, which has 45,000 seats; great training school for **gladiators**; house of Bruttius Praesens; central theatrical storehouse; Shepherd's Fountain; Baths of Titus and Trajan; Portico of Livia; camp of the sailors of the Miseum fleet; 12 crossroad shrines; 2,757 **apartment blocks**; 60 private **houses**; 18 storehouses; 80 **baths**; 65 fountains; 16 bakeries.'

The catalogues for each district showed that Rome had, at this time, 28 libraries, 8 **bridges**, 11 **forums**, 10 **basilicas**, 11 major public baths, 19 **aqueducts** and 29 **roads**. Romans were talented engineers and architects. One architect, **Vitruvius**, wrote a manual of how to plan and build all types of Roman constructions – even towns. Builders were also able to employ large, cheap labour forces – mostly **slaves**.

Burials and tombstones

When a Roman died, the **family** not only cried but beat their chests and went about with torn clothes and their hair in a mess. For the rich, funerals were elaborate and costly; those less wealthy could join a funeral club and pay monthly dues so that they might be buried properly.

If the family could afford a special funeral ceremony, it was a more complicated affair than is usual today. The body would be laid out on a bed at home. At each corner, torches and candles would be burning. Pine cones, which were a symbol of eternal life, or small pine branches might also be burned to give off a rich smell. Perhaps this was to hide the smell of the corpse, which was expected to lie in the house for a week. On the day of the funeral, the person who had died would be carried on a litter to the cemetery. If the person was important, the body might be carried to the **forum** and a public speech, called a *laudatio*, was made about his or her life. The funeral procession continued on to

the cemetery with trumpet and flute players in the lead. There might also be torch bearers, professional mourners and **actors** representing the dead person's relatives walking in front of the mourning relatives.

The body might then be cremated and the ashes put into a special jar. Burial, rather than cremation, became more common in the 2nd century AD. Cemeteries had to be, by law, outside the limits or walls of the town or city. If the family could afford it, a tombstone would be made with an inscription and perhaps a portrait. The very rich had a large family vault (a mausoleum) or a tomb, called a *columbarium*, for the jars full of the ashes of their cremated relatives. In **Rome**, and in some other cities, underground burial chambers, called **catacombs**, were cut into the rock. It was here that many **Christians** were buried.

The Romans believed that the dead went to live in the underworld with the **gods** of the dead (the Manes). Offerings, in the form of wine poured out or food left by the graveside, were made to these gods at certain times. The first time was nine days after burial and then at special festivals throughout the year.

Below: Part of the tomb of two freedmen (former slaves) who died near Rome around 20–1 BC. The carving above their heads and on the right reveal what work they did in life – one was a blacksmith, the other a carpenter. On the left are pictured the rod and staffs used in the official ceremony to free the two men.

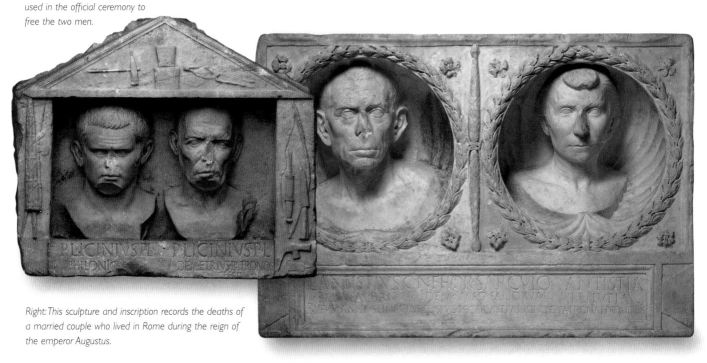

Right: This sculpture and inscription records the deaths of a married couple who lived in Rome during the reign of the emperor Augustus.

Below: This stone coffin was found in London and was made for a twelve-year-old boy who died in the 4th century AD. His skeleton was found inside a lead inner coffin. The boy's body had been buried in lime, inside the lead coffin, which helped to reduce the smell and preserve his remains. The boy's portrait is carved on the side of the stone coffin, which probably stood against a wall in the cemetery.

Above: These two tombstones are from the Roman city of Lincoln in Britain. On the left is the tombstone of a soldier called Gaius Saufeius, who came from Macedonia in Greece. He served in the 9th legion and died around AD 60, aged forty, after twenty-two years in the army. On the other (above right) is the record of Titus Valerius Pudens, who died in AD 76 aged thirty. Pudens came from the colony of Savaria in the province of Pannonia Superior (now modern Hungary).

C

Calendar

Even before the **Etruscans** took over **Rome** a calendar was in use. It was based on the moon and divided the year into ten months. Later, two more months were added. The year had 355 days in it. To make the length of the year correct they added an extra month of twenty-two or twenty-three days every two years. The Roman year began on 1 March but later, in 153 BC, it was changed to start on 1 January.

By the time of **Julius Caesar** the calendar was in chaos because no extra month had been added since 58 BC. The Roman year was now ninety days too short. Caesar decided to put matters right, and in 46 BC he declared the year to have 365 days. Actually he knew that it was slightly longer than that, so he added an extra day to February every fourth year – our Leap Year.

The new calendar, called the Julian Calendar after Caesar's family name, began on 1 January 45 BC. Although some changes were made to this calendar by Pope Gregory XIII in 1582, the Roman calendar is still the one we use today. The Romans had an eight-day week – seven working days and one market day.

The Roman months

Januarius – named after Janus the god of beginnings.
Februarius – from the word meaning 'to clean ceremonially'.
Martialis – after the god of war, **Mars**.
Aprilis – from the word meaning 'the opening of flowers'.
Maius – a month sacred to the goddess of warm weather, Maia.
Junius – the month of the **goddess Juno**.
Julius – originally called Quintilis, the fifth month, but it was renamed in honour of Julius Caesar.

Augustus – once called Sextilis, the sixth month, but it was renamed after the emperor **Augustus**.
September, October, November and *December* – from the words for the Roman **numbers** seven, eight, nine and ten.

Canals

The Romans used water routes wherever possible to travel and to move goods. Moving goods by water was cheaper than by land. Inland waterways, like rivers, were ideal but their engineers also constructed waterways – canals. We know of several canal-building schemes, including some in **Britain**, linking rivers to provide longer waterway routes. We do not know if the Romans used locks on their canals, but they certainly had the engineering skill and knowledge to do so. We know that some canal and river traffic was organized by the **army**. There is a record left on **Hadrian's Wall** of a unit of bargemen recruited from the river Tigris in Mesopotamia working on the river Tyne.

These two figures are part of a large floor mosaic (see page 142) from the villa at Lullingstone in Britain. Each corner of the mosaic showed a different season of the year. What you see here is Spring (top) with a swallow on her shoulder (the arrival of swallows in Europe is said to be the start of summer) and Autumn (above) with a garland of corn (gathered as part of the autumn harvest).

Part of the ruins of the city of Carthage showing the Roman baths that were begun by Hadrian but not completed until AD 146.

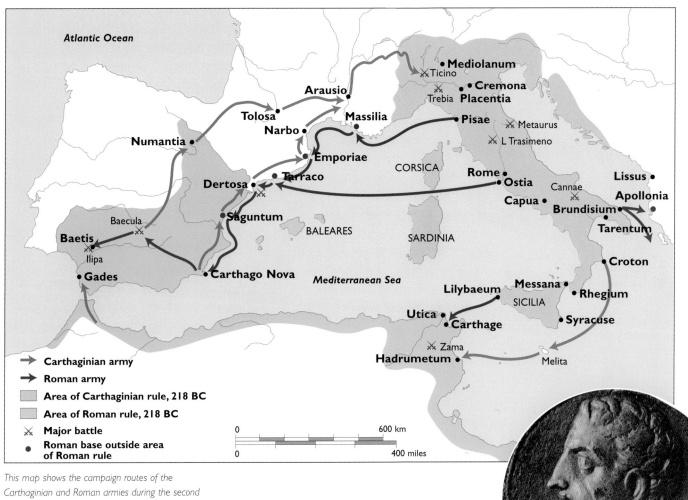

This map shows the campaign routes of the Carthaginian and Roman armies during the second war with Carthage.

This coin, which was minted in 230–220 BC by the powerful Barcid family of Carthage, is thought to show a portrait of the family's most famous member – Hannibal.

Carthage and Hannibal

Carthage is situated on the coast of north **Africa**, in the country that is now Tunisia. The earliest **settlement** was established in around 800 BC and it became the capital of the Carthaginians. It was an impressive place and the Roman historian **Livy** tells us that the city was large, with protective walls that stretched for nearly 33 km (more than 20 miles).

The Carthaginians were a seafaring people and they had a large **navy** and they proved to be the most difficult of all the peoples the Romans had to conquer in order to establish themselves as the most powerful nation in the Mediterranean region. **Rome**'s first war with Carthage began in 264 BC, when a Carthaginian force occupied the town of Messana, on the island of Sicily. In response to this, the Romans sent two **legions** and defeated them. They then built a fleet of **ships** in preparation for a full-scale war, which did not end until 241 BC when the Romans occupied Sicily and made it a **province** of the **empire**

Hamilcar was the general in charge of the Carthaginian army in this first war with the Romans. In 237 BC he led an **army** into Spain (then called **Hispania**) to conquer new territories and also to defend the existing Carthaginian settlements. At this time his son, called Hannibal, was about nine years old. Hamilcar made him swear an oath on an

On this, the reverse side of a coin minted in about 230 BC in Carthage, you can see a war elephant, as used by Hannibal in his war against the Romans.

altar to be the enemy of Rome as soon as he was old enough. Hannibal took control of the Carthaginian forces in Spain in 221 BC, when he was twenty-five years old.

The Romans sent two armies to fight Hannibal, but he outwitted them both and made a forced march into Italy, crossing the Alps. His army was huge – about 40,000 soldiers in total. His force also included thirty-seven war elephants.

Crossing the Alps was very difficult, and only 26,000 men and twelve elephants survived the ordeal. To make up these losses, Hannibal recruited large numbers of Celtic warriors on the way and defeated the Romans in several major battles.

Eventually a newly appointed Roman commander, Publius Cornelius Scipio, engaged the Carthaginians and managed to defeat them in 202 BC.

Hannibal himself escaped but later committed suicide in 183 BC rather than be taken prisoner by the Romans. Despite the loss of their commander, the Carthaginians fought the Romans, and a third and final war began in 149 BC. It ended with Scipio occupying Carthage and making slaves of all of the city's 50,000 inhabitants. Carthaginian territory became a Roman province. The city was destroyed and a *colonia*, a new colony, was established there (see **Cities and new towns**).

Catacombs

Roman law allowed the dead to be buried only outside towns and cities, usually along main **roads** (see **Burials and tombstones**). Catacombs are burial places dug into soft rock underground. These cemeteries have been found outside several Roman cities, including **Alexandria**, but the largest and most famous are along the Via Appia, one of the main routes into **Rome**. Many others

This wall painting is in the underground crypt of the Church of St Sebastian on the Via Appia in Rome. It shows the way coffins were stored on ledges cut into the rock.

These two cavalrymen are preparing for a parade or a display. They have decorated helmets with face masks (see page 145). The one on his horse is carrying a standard in the form of a dragon with a tail made from pieces of coloured cloth.

An artist's impression of auxiliary Roman soldiers showing cavalry troopers armed and ready to fight. Their weapons are long swords and spears, and they carry oval-shaped shields.

have been discovered and in total they stretch for 550 km (340 miles). Underground tunnels lead to rooms with holes cut into the rock walls to hold the bodies. They were originally used for the general population, but from the 2nd century AD onwards they were used by **Christians** to bury their dead, and the walls were painted with scenes from the Bible. Many Christians who were executed during the persecutions were buried in catacombs.

Catullus

The poet Catullus was born in Verona in Italy in about 84 BC but moved to **Rome** as a young man. Although more than a hundred of his poems survive, we know very little about him. His poems tell us

that he served on the staff of a governor of one of Rome's **provinces**.

Cavalry

During the **republic**, Roman commanders such as **Julius Caesar** employed groups of horsemen supplied by local chieftains. In the period of the **empire** these cavalry units were organized into regiments (*alae*) of 500 men. Some cavalry units were very lightly armed, carrying only spears. Others were heavily armed with spears and long swords and were protected with helmets and body armour (see **Weapons and armour**). The emperor **Trajan** had twenty-four units of cavalry (about 17,000 men) in his army of about 60,000 when he invaded Dacia in 101 AD.

The tombstone of a centurion, Marcus Favonius Facilis, who died in Colchester, Britain, in about AD 48. He served in the 20th legion and was almost certainly one of the soldiers who took part in the emperor Claudius's invasion of Britain. Facilis is shown wearing the uniform of a centurion with a moulded breast plate, overlapping strips of metal like a skirt and leg guards. He has a short sword and dagger and carries a stick made of vine wood. It symbolizes the centurion's right to flog the men under his command.

The excitement and danger of chariot racing are shown in this carving. Four chariots are racing around the central barrier of the circus. In the centre of this picture you can see four of the seven great wooden balls. The Romans called these 'ova' (eggs). They showed the crowd which of the seven laps was in progress.

Centurions

Officers who commanded the units of eighty men (called a *centuria*) were called centurions. They were very experienced legionary soldiers (see **Legions and legionaries**). They wore special armour and carried a cane made of vine wood to punish the soldiers they commanded. Centurions were well known for being brutal. Other, junior, officers reported to a centurion. The *optio* was the centurion's second in command and below him was the standard bearer (**signifer**).

Chariot racing

One of the sports the Romans enjoyed most was chariot racing, perhaps because it was exciting and dangerous. Many towns had their own stadium where four teams – wearing red, blue, green and

white colours – raced round a central barrier with their light chariots pulled by four horses. The biggest stadium of all was in **Rome** and was called the **Circus Maximus**. Spectators placed bets on which team would win. There were seven laps and each race covered about 6.5 km (4 miles). It was usual to have twenty-four races a day. Charioteers could become very rich and some even had their own fan clubs. One charioteer, called Diocles, had his career recorded on a monument in Rome, which tells us that he came from Spain (**Hispania**), drove for twenty-four years and won 1,462 races, exceeding the record of any other charioteer.

'I wouldn't mind if the spectators went to see the speed of the horses or the skill of the charioteers. But all they support is the colour of the driver's tunic. If they swapped colours in mid-race, I swear they'd follow the colours and change their support too.'
Pliny the Younger

This glass beaker from Colchester in Britain may have been a souvenir of a day at the chariot races in the 1st century AD.

This domestic beaker from the 2nd century AD shows four chariots racing around it and was also found in Colchester.

Children

In Roman society boys were considered more useful than girls. Boys and men had more rights and privileges than girls and women. A boy could expect to be better educated and could take part in public life, serve in the army and had the protection of more laws than girls had. When a boy 'came of age' at sixteen, he dedicated his *bulla* (the lucky charm he had worn around his neck since he was born) and his **toga** *praetexta* (a special boy's garment) to the **household gods**. In contrast, a girl dedicated her **toys** to the household gods when she got married.

These customs, however, really applied only to well-off children. Most people in the Roman world were not rich. The children of poor families could not expect to be educated, and boys and girls were sent out to work as early as possible. They might be apprenticed to a trade, perhaps for a year, or do the same work as their parents.

Christianity

Many people across the Roman world were Christians, although they often had to worship in secret because of persecution. Because of their religion, Christians would not recognize the **gods and goddesses** of the Roman state or make **sacrifices** to them. Because Christians refused to recognize the official Roman religion they suffered persecution. Christians chose to bury their dead in their own cemeteries on the roads leading out of Rome.

Christians are associated with the **catacombs** on the Via Appia in **Rome** near the Church of St Sebastian, and many Christians were buried in these underground chambers. However, the catacombs were used well before the Christian

This is a marble bust of a young girl from Italy, carved in the 3rd century AD. Her hairstyle is interesting because over her own long tresses is a wig with waved hair parted in the middle.

These rings could be used to stamp a wax seal. The design (also shown opposite) is reversed on the rings so that it appears the right way around in the wax.

Left: The central part of a 4th-century floor mosaic from a villa at Hinton St Mary in Dorset, Britain. It shows the head of Christ with the first two letters of his name in Greek – Chi (X) and Rho (P) – behind his head. On each side of his head are pomegranates, which were considered symbols of eternal life. You can see this floor mosaic in full on page 95.

Above: This wall painting, from a villa at Lullingstone in Kent, Britain, has been reconstructed from fragments excavated by archaeologists. It is dated to the late 4th century and shows six figures in tunics with beaded sashes in the form of a cross and their arms outstretched in prayer. The painting is on the wall of a room that the owners of the villa converted into a Christian chapel.

period. These were underground tombs hollowed out of the soft rock. It was here that illegal religious services were held. After centuries of persecution, the emperor **Constantine** I passed a decree, in AD 313, tolerating Christianity. Christianity was then adopted as the state religion, although many people chose to continue worshipping the old gods. Christian churches have been discovered in many Roman towns all over the **empire**. There were even chapels in some Roman **villas**.

Cicero

Cicero was one of **Rome**'s best orators (public speakers). As a lawyer he was famous for his speeches against Verres, the terrible governor of Sicily who had stolen from and murdered many of that island's inhabitants. Cicero also published a number of books, including nearly 800 of his letters, as well as books dealing with public speaking. He was the holder of various political offices, including the most important of all as **consul**. Cicero sided with **Pompey** in the **civil war** against **Julius Caesar**, for which he was eventually put to death by Octavian (later known as **Augustus**).

This fired-clay (or terracotta) plaque was originally part of a series that decorated the upper walls of a room or a shrine. It shows a charioteer whipping on his horses at the most dangerous part of each lap. He is about to wheel around the ends of the central barrier (the 'spina'). The ends of this barrier, called the 'metae', are clearly marked by three pointed columns. Look above the horses and you can see the plaque-maker's name – Anniae Arescusa.

Circus Maximus

The largest stadium for **chariot racing** in the Roman world was the Circus Maximus in **Rome**. The huge building was 600 m (nearly 2,000 ft) long, but it started out as a simple race track. It was gradually added to and rebuilt so that 100,000 spectators could watch the sport by the 1st century BC. Several **emperors** enlarged it, and the emperor **Nero** surpassed them all when he rebuilt it to hold 250,000 people in AD 64. Despite the death of 13,000 spectators when temporary wooden seating collapsed in the 3rd century AD, it was enlarged again in the 4th century to hold an incredible 350,000 people.

Cities and new towns

Anyone living in the Roman **empire** would expect to see towns and cities with much the same facilities. When new towns were built in the **provinces**, the townspeople would want the types of **buildings** and amenities they had seen, or had heard about, in the capital of the empire, **Rome**. The town council, called the *ordo*, governed the affairs of the town. **Officials** were elected or appointed to deal with matters such as taxes, town planning, public buildings, **roads**, entertainment and the **water supply**.

Towns were laid out in a regular way, with streets crossing at right angles to form blocks called *insulae* (see **Apartment blocks**). Many Roman towns and cities were built in places that were already established **settlements** – the Greek city of **Athens**, for example. Others, such as **Colchester** in **Britain**, were created where Roman **forts** had been built to conquer a new territory. New towns were quickly built once a province had been occupied.

There were three types of new towns. A *colonia* was a town established by moving Roman citizens into a new territory. A *colonia* was also a place for retired soldiers. A *municipium* was a town that had been given a charter allowing the townspeople to organize their own affairs and set up a town council. A *civitas* was a town established as the main centre of a tribal area. These towns organized some of their own affairs, but control was really in the hands of the governor of the province.

Civil war

In the 1st century BC there was a struggle for power as **Rome** began to change after its conquests around the Mediterranean. By 49 BC **Julius Caesar** had become the most powerful person in Rome. He had won new **provinces** for the **republic** and was governor of the province in northern Italy. His rival, **Pompey**, persuaded the **senate** to order him to disband his **armies**. Caesar refused and crossed the River Rubicon, between his province and Italy proper, and declared war on the senate.

He pursued Pompey's army to Brundisium, in southern Italy, but he did not have enough **ships** to follow him to **Greece**. Caesar turned back and went to Spain to defeat Pompey's armies there. The following year, 48 BC, he led his army to Greece and defeated Pompey's forces at the Battle of Pharsalus. Pompey's army then fled to **Egypt**. In 47 BC Caesar returned to Italy, but he continued his pursuit of Pompey's armies and defeated one in North **Africa** in 46 BC. In the following year Caesar won a final battle in Spain.

Julius Caesar was now in complete control of the government and the armies of the Roman state and he eventually declared himself '**dictator** for life' in 44 BC. It was obvious that Caesar wanted

A road in the city of Ephesus (in modern-day Turkey) with a temple to the emperor Hadrian on one side. Ephesus became the most important city in the province of Asia.

to see an end to republican government and wanted the supreme title of *rex* ('king'). The aristocracy in Rome, led by Marcus **Brutus** and Gaius Cassius, decided to assassinate him. Ignoring all the signs and warnings of the prophets that he would be murdered on the Ides of March (15 March), Caesar entered the senate building on that day and was indeed stabbed to death.

Caesar's death did not end the power struggle. Another civil war broke out between his adopted son and heir, Octavian, and Marcus Antonius (usually called **Mark Antony**). Eventually the Roman world was divided between them, with Antony ruling from **Alexandria** in Egypt with his lover, Queen **Cleopatra**. The Roman state declared war on Antony, and Octavian won the final battle at Actium in Greece. Octavian was now totally in control and was eventually given the title of Augustus – and became the emperor **Augustus**.

Claudius

Claudius, born in Lugdunum (now Lyon in **Gaul**, had noble parents. His father was the son of the emperor **Augustus**'s wife **Livia** and his mother the daughter of **Mark Antony**. He did not imagine that he would one day become **emperor**. In AD 41, when Claudius was fifty years old, Caligula, the emperor at the time, and Claudius's nephew, was murdered. The emperor's bodyguard, the praetorian guard, was hunting down Caligula's assassins when soldier came across Claudius hiding behind a curtain, terrified. The soldiers hauled him off to their camp and declared him emperor.

Although Claudius had no military experience, he decided to invade **Britai** and stayed with his invading army for sixteen days. By the end of his reign five new **provinces** had been added to the Roman **empire**, although Claudius took part only in the British campaign.

Claudius was well educated and intelligent. He wrote histories of the **Etruscans** and the **Cathaginians**. He also completed a number of building projects, including two **aqueducts** for **Rome**, the draining of a huge lake to create farmland and a new harbour at **Ostia**.

This bronze head of the emperor Claudius is from the 1st century AD. The head was found in a river in Suffolk and it may have been thrown there by the rebels, led by Queen Boudica, in AD 60.

Claudius married four times. He divorced his first two wives, and his third wife, Messalina, had many affairs and was probably plotting against him. She was executed. His last wife, Agrippina, poisoned him in AD 54 after ensuring that her son by a previous marriage, **Nero**, became the next emperor instead of Claudius's son, Britannicus.

Cleopatra

The name Cleopatra was given to many of the princesses of the Ptolemies, a Greek family who ruled ancient **Egypt** for 300 years. The most famous was Queen Cleopatra VII, who ruled with her half-brother, Ptolemy XIII. He drove Cleopatra out but she was supported by **Julius Caesar**, who made Cleopatra queen of Egypt after Ptolemy was killed. Cleopatra claimed her son born after Caesar left Egypt was his and named him Caesarion.

This portrait of Queen Cleopatra of Egypt appears on a coin. It looks as if Cleopatra inherited the hooked nose of her father, Ptolemy XII Auletes.

Mark Antony, who fought against Octavian in the **civil war**, had his base in the coastal city of **Alexandria** in Egypt. He fell in love with Cleopatra and allowed her and her son to be declared joint rulers of Egypt and Cyprus. When Antony lost the final battle with Octavian (later **Augustus**) the lovers committed suicide – Antony stabbed himself and died in her arms. Later Cleopatra, in AD 30, allowed a deadly snake to bite her rather than be captured by the Romans.

Clothes

Roman clothes were simpler than most people wear today. Clothes were made from wool or linen, although the rich might also have worn silk garments. Cloth was dyed in a variety of different colours and shades – white, black, yellow, green, blue, red and purple. Purple was one of the most expensive of these colours. The most famous purple dye came from Tyre, in Phoenicia, where the colour was extracted from shell-fish. **Underclothes** were also worn.

The tunic was the standard garment for men. It was simply made by folding a piece of cloth, sewing the sides and leaving a hole for the head. Another common garment was the cloak for outside wear. In some parts of the Roman world men also wore trousers.

Probably the most well-known Roman garment known today is the **toga**. This was an outer garment worn only by men who were Roman citizens. It was a semicircular piece of cloth, often 5 m (16½ ft) wide, which had to be draped over the body.

Women also wore tunics, sometimes an under-tunic as well. On top, a woman would wear a dress called a *stola*. It was worn by respectable married women and was a long, loose-fitting garment that was gathered at the hips and under the bust. When leaving the house, a woman would wear a *palla*, which was a rectangle of cloth draped over her head and covering her body from shoulder to knee.

Men and women wore hats, but respectable women in towns always kept their head covered, usually with the *palla*. Fashionable women also carried parasols to keep off the sun. Working men and women, especially on **farms**, wore straw hats. Roman **shoes** and boots have been found by archaeologists, and **statues** usually show examples of these. Sandals were very popular.

Babies were wrapped in swaddling clothes to keep them from moving, but older **children** generally wore the same kinds of clothes as their parents.

A fragment of a wall painting from the time of the emperor Augustus. The woman is standing on a balcony looking down, perhaps into her garden, and drinking from a cup. She is wearing a loose-fitting tunic gathered at the waist and a hat made from the same light green material as her tunic.

This is what archaeologists think Colchester may have looked like in AD 250. The main road from London enters on the left and passes through an elaborate arched gateway, thought to celebrate the triumph of the successful invasion of Britain in AD 43. A wall of stone and tiles surrounds the town, which was rectangular in shape. Almost at the end of the main street is a large courtyard and, in the centre, the temple to the emperor Claudius. On its left is the town's theatre.

'It seemed an easy matter for the Britons to destroy the colony since it hadn't a single fortification to defend it. The Roman generals cared more for amenities and show than for what was really needed. The town was destroyed by fire and the inhabitants put to death. The temple of Claudius held out for two days but was then taken.'
Tacitus describing the destruction of Colchester by Queen Boudica in AD 60

Cohorts

A cohort is a body of troops. There were ten cohorts in a Roman **legion**. The first cohort consisted of the best troops and contained about 600 men, while the other nine cohorts had about 500 men in each. A cohort was divided into six *centuriae* ('centuries' of about eighty soldiers), and each was commanded by an officer called a **centurion**.

Colchester

Colchester was the capital of pre-Roman **Britain**. The emperor **Claudius** marched to this city at the head of his **army**, complete with war elephants, during the Roman **invasion** of AD 43. A **fort** was built at the site of the modern town, but in AD 49 a new town for retired soldiers was established on the site (see **Cities and new towns**). Claudius named the

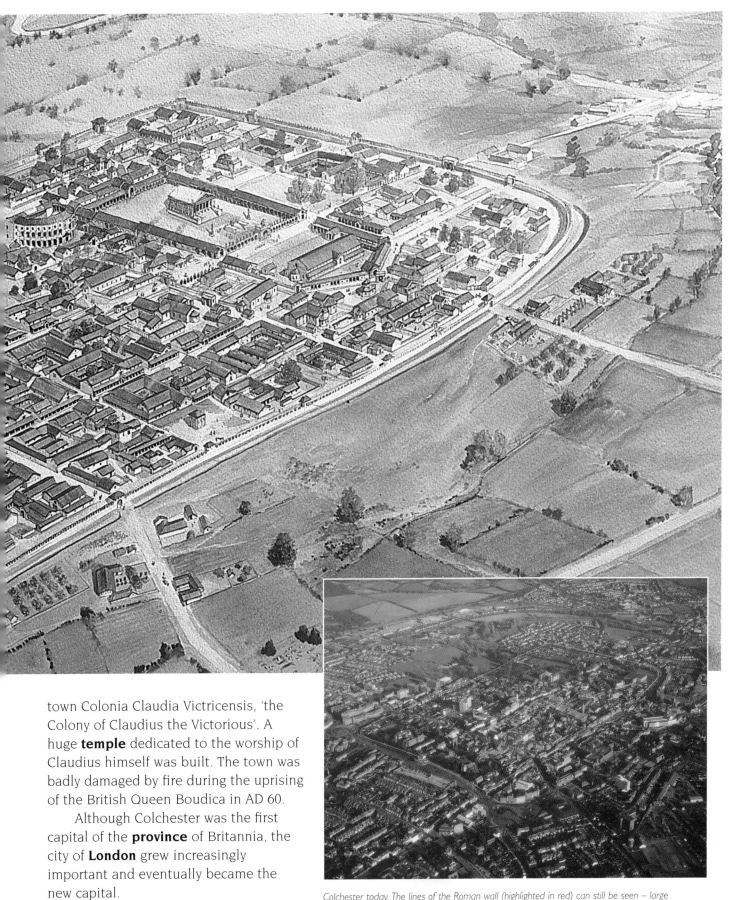

town Colonia Claudia Victricensis, 'the Colony of Claudius the Victorious'. A huge **temple** dedicated to the worship of Claudius himself was built. The town was badly damaged by fire during the uprising of the British Queen Boudica in AD 60.

Although Colchester was the first capital of the **province** of Britannia, the city of **London** grew increasingly important and eventually became the new capital.

Colchester today. The lines of the Roman wall (highlighted in red) can still be seen – large portions of it survive – along with the high street, first laid out by Roman surveyors.

Colosseum

The proper name for the Colosseum was the Amphitheatrum Flavium. The massive building was begun by the emperor **Vespasian**, whose family name was Flavius, but it was not finally completed until AD 80, during the reign of his son, Titus. The Colosseum got its name from a colossal statue of the emperor **Nero** that stood nearby.

The largest of all Roman **amphitheatres**, it is 188 x 156 m (617 x 512 ft) and, according to Roman records, could hold between 60,000 and 70,000 spectators who poured in through its 80 entrances to see the games. **Officials** and high-ranking spectators occupied the first two tiers, nearest the action in the arena

This coin from the time of the emperor Titus was minted in Rome in AD 80–81 and shows the Colosseum packed with spectators.

'What nation is so remote, Emperor, or so barbarous that someone hasn't come from it to watch the games in your city? There are farmers from the Balkans here, natives from southern Russia bred on horses' blood, people who drink the Nile's waters and even those from far away Britain. Arabs, people from the shores of the Red Sea, as well as those from southern Turkey, have hurried here and German tribesmen and Ethiopians each with their own peculiar hairstyles.'

Martial – part of a poem addressed to the emperor Titus on the opening of the Colosseum in AD 80 (the sand-covered floor where the games took place). Then came a tier for the middle classes and the highest tier was for lower classes, **slaves**, **women** and **children**.

To shade the spectators from the burning sun, a huge awning was pulled up by a squadron of imperial sailors detailed to the task to cover the whole building. **Gladiators** entered the arena through gates below the seats. Wild **animals** in cages were lifted by hoists from rooms under the arena.

Columella

Columella came from Gades (now Cadiz) in Spain. He retired from the **army** and became a farmer in Italy. He published books on how to run farming estates and on the cultivation of trees and shrubs. (see **Farms**).

Left: The outside surviving wall of the Colosseum in Rome. Much of the stone of the building was taken for other constructions right up until the 18th century, when Pope Benedict XIV declared the amphitheatre a place sacred to the Christians who, according to the Pope, had been slaughtered there.

Below: Inside the Colosseum. Although the seating has been taken away you can still get a good idea of the four tiers – from officials to the lowest classes and slaves.

A portrait of Constantine the Great on a silver coin minted in Trier, Germany, in AD 306–7.

Constantine the Great

Constantine I was born at Naissus in the **province** of Moesia (now Serbia). He was proclaimed **emperor** by his troops in **York** in **Britain** in AD 306 on the death of his father, Constantinus. When the emperor Maximinus Daia died in AD 313, two men controlled the Roman **empire**: Constantine claimed the western provinces, including Italy and north **Africa** and Licinius took the east.

At first, the two men each governed their respective parts of the empire. Then Constantine invaded Licinius's provinces and finally, by AD 324, defeated all the opposing **armies**. He had already moved his capital to Byzantium (now Istanbul in Turkey) and renamed it after himself – **Constantinople**, which means the city of Constantine, or 'New Rome'. He was known throughout his united empire as Constantine the Great. He introduced **Christianity** as the official religion of **Rome** and was baptized into the Christian faith shortly before his death in AD 337.

Constantinople

Constantine I (known as **Constantine the Great**) made the ancient city of Byzantium, on the entrance to the Black Sea, his new capital on 11 May AD 330. He named it Constantinople after himself – the city of Constantine. As the **empire** grew, so did its capital city within the huge defensive walls built by the **emperor** Theodosius in the 5th century AD. By this time, the huge city had 4,388 **houses**, 11 imperial palaces, 14 churches, five markets and eight public **baths**. The eastern Roman empire, also called the Byzantine empire, lasted until the Ottoman Turks conquered Constantinople on 23 May 1453. It is now the Turkish city of Istanbul.

Consuls

The two most important **officials** in the Roman government were called consuls. They were the heads of government and were also in charge of the army, but for one year only. It was said that **Romulus**, the founder of **Rome**, decided on two chief officials to stop one man from declaring himself an all-powerful king. The Romans named their years after the names of the consuls.

Corinth

Corinth was a wealthy city in ancient **Greece**. In the middle of the 2nd century BC, Corinth fought against the Romans. The Roman **consul** Lucius Mummius was sent to Greece with a large fleet and an army. He burned the city and made all its inhabitants **slaves**. **Julius Caesar** chose the site of Corinth as a *colonia* (see **Cities and new towns**) to settle retired soldiers from Italy. He rebuilt the city, and it finally became the capital of the Roman **province**. One of the sights of modern Greece is the Corinth **Canal**, which joins the Gulf of Corinth to the Aegean Sea. Julius Caesar wanted to build a canal here, the emperor Caligula surveyed the site, and the emperor **Nero** actually set 6,000 Jewish war slaves to work on it. The modern canal was constructed in 1893.

Above: These are the remains of the centre of the Greek city of Corinth. On the other side of the 'agora' (the Greek word for forum) are the columns of the temple of Apollo.

High, strong walls, fortified by enormous towers, surrounded and protected the city of Constantinople.

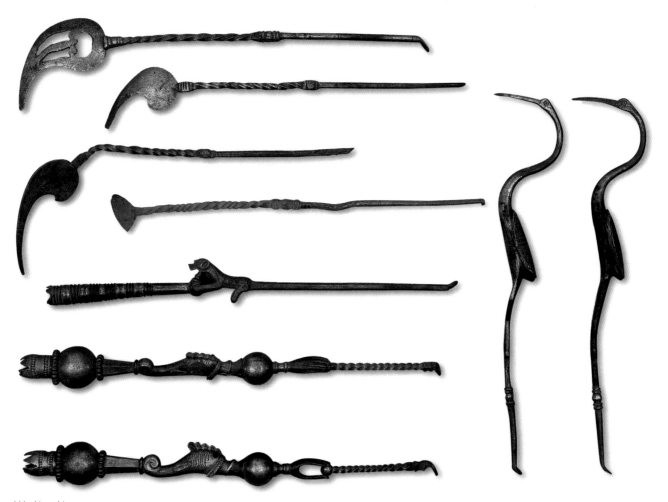

These odd-looking objects were buried by their owner for safety in eastern Britain in the 5th century AD at the end of the Roman period. They are all made from silver and were used for applying cosmetics and for teeth cleaning. The top four on the left were used as toothpicks with little scoops at the other end, perhaps for cleaning ears or taking cosmetics from small glass bottles. Below them are three objects that probably held little brushes at the left ends for applying powder. The scoop at the other end was perhaps for make-up. The remaining two objects on the right are beautifully made toothpicks in the shape of a long-legged bird called an ibis.

Cosmetics

Women, and sometimes men as well, wore cosmetics. Chalk or white lead was popular for face powder; red ochre could be crushed and mixed to colour the lips; and ash was used for the outside of the eyes. The poet **Ovid** gives the ingredients for a cream to make the skin softer, which included crushed barley, eggs, the ground-up horn of a stag, bulbs from the narcissus plant and honey.

The tools used for personal cleaning and applying cosmetics shown above are particularly fine examples, but many people carried a little set attached to a ring. The set might have included a pair of tweezers, an ear-scoop and a nail-cleaner. In the home there would be a polished bronze mirror so that you could check on your appearance.

Crops

The Romans grew a variety of **crops** throughout their many **provinces**. Wheat, barley and rye were most important as basic food sources for the huge population in the cities. The Romans liked vegetables and grew a great variety – for example, carrots, lettuce, cabbage, parsnips, turnips, peas, radishes, onions, leeks, cucumbers and marrows. **Olives** were grown in huge quantities, both to eat and to make into oil. Grapes grew in many parts of the Roman world for **wine**. Fruit was imported into the towns and sold at markets and in **shops** – for example, apples, figs, cherries, peaches and plums. All sorts of wild **food** were gathered – nuts, berries, strawberries and crab apples, for example, as well as herbs.

Cursus publicus

The emperor **Augustus** established an official courier service called the *cursus publicus* to take documents, information and people travelling on official business across the empire. Relays of horses were stabled between 10 and 25 km (6 and 16 miles) apart on the main routes. **Officials** might be transported on an open carriage drawn by three horses. There were also resthouses called *mansiones*, for overnight stops every 32 or 48 km (20 or 30 miles).

One of the best-preserved *mansiones* in **Britain** is at a small **settlement** at Wall, called Letocetum by the Romans. The settlement was built on the main road, which ran from the original landing place of the emperor **Claudius**'s **invasion** force in AD 43 up through the midlands of the **province** to Wales. The most important buildings of this small settlement are the mansion and **baths**. Rooms for guests were on the ground and upper floors, grouped around an open courtyard.

Three important Roman documents hold clues to where these official resting places might be. The Antonine Itinerary is a 3rd-century AD list of roads and staging posts throughout the **empire** based on information from a map of the empire set up in **Rome** under Augustus. The second is the Tabula Peutingeriana, which is a map of the empire originally drawn in the 3rd century AD and revised in the 5th century. The copies that exist today were made in the 13th century. The last is a map of the empire from the 7th century called the Ravenna Cosmography. It lists about 5,000 place names from colonies to the smallest settlements.

An artist's impression of the courtyard leading to the guests' rooms in the mansio at Wall in Britain.

D

Democracy

The word 'democracy' was taken from the ancient **Greeks**. It describes the type of system in which the state is governed by politicians and **officials** elected by citizens. Once the last Roman king, **Tarquin the Proud**, had been thrown out in 509 BC, the people of **Rome** established a form of government that they called a **republic**.

Diana

The name of this **goddess** probably means 'bright one'. Diana, known as Artemis, the twin sister of **Apollo**, by the Greeks, was a wood-spirit often worshipped as a huntress. Images of Diana often show her with her hunting hound. She was believed to have powers of fertility.

This coin of Julius Caesar has the words PERPETVO CAESAR DICT around his head, meaning 'Caesar Dictator for Life'. On the reverse of coins minted during the republic are abbreviations, as here, for the name of the official responsible for issuing the coin.

Dictator

In times of crisis a **consul** could name a *dictator* for the **senate** to approve. This man could hold the post for a maximum of six months. **Julius Caesar** declared himself 'dictator for life', which was an illegal act. In the times of the **emperors**, **officials** were still elected but sometimes their jobs changed.

This statue of the goddess Diana was found at Seville in Spain. She is dressed for hunting. Unfortunately her lower arms are now missing.

Dio Cassius

Dio Cassius worked as a lawyer and held a number of political offices, including that of **consul**. When he retired after a long public career, he spent ten years collecting information and then twelve years writing his *History of Rome*. The eighty books that make up this great work cover the period from **Rome**'s legendary beginnings to AD 229 (he died in about AD 230).

Diocletian

For fifty years after the murder of the emperor Alexander Severus in AD 235 there was chaos in the Roman **empire**. There were twenty **emperors** and five who reigned over a break-away empire in **Gaul** for fifteen years.

This period of chaos was brought to a conclusion by Diocletian. He came from a humble family in the **province** of Dalmatia (probably near the city of Spalato, now **Split**). His father may have been a secretary or even a freed **slave**. He went into the **army** and served in the guard of the emperor Numerian.

Diocletian was declared emperor by the army in AD 284. The following year he chose to rule with a junior colleague, a trusted army commander called Maximian. Diocletian was the senior man and made all the important decisions. Jointly they campaigned against enemies, bands of robbers and contenders for imperial power. One of these, Carausius, the commander of the Roman fleet in the North Sea, declared himself emperor in **Britain** in AD 287.

Diocletian considered that the idea of having joint emperors was a successful system and decided that both he and Maximian would appoint a junior colleague each. These colleagues would become joint emperors when Diocletian and Maximian eventually died.

Diocletian made a fundamental change to the way the empire was organized. He grouped provinces together into twelve large 'dioceses', each governed by a 'vicar'. These new-style governors did not command the army, as had been the case in the past, and this change made rebellion against the emperor very difficult to carry out. Diocletian also introduced a system of fixed prices for goods, services and the amount of money people earned across the empire.

It was during Diocletian's reign that **Christians** were viciously persecuted. In AD 297 or 298 he signed a decree that all soldiers and civil servants should make **sacrifices** to the traditional **gods and goddesses** and the emperor of **Rome**. Those who refused to obey were forced to quit their posts.

In AD 303 an edict was issued to destroy all Christian churches and scriptures. All Christian clergy were to be arrested and imprisoned. Any people who refused to sacrifice to Roman gods were tortured and killed. Christians were killed in large numbers, and some were even thrown to wild **animals**, such as lions, for the entertainment of cheering spectators.

Rome itself began to decline in importance and became far less crucial to the government of the empire. Diocletian went to Rome only once, in AD 303. When he and his joint emperor, Maximian, abdicated together in favour of their junior colleagues, Diocletian retired to the palace he had built in Split, where he died in AD 311.

A coin showing the emperor Diocletian, minted in Carthage in the early 4th century AD to commemorate his retirement. The coin uses the word FELICISSIMO, which means 'most fortunate', to describe him.

Prices in denarii
Ordinary wine for 1 sextarius 8
Egyptian beer for 1 sextarius 2
Honey, best quality 1 sextarius 24
10 Dormice 40
Soldier's boots 100

Daily wages in denarii
Farm labourer 25
Picture painter 150
Camel driver 25
Sewer cleaner 25

Monthly wages in denarii
Elementary teacher 25
Lawyer 250

From Diocletian's *Edict on Maximum Prices* (for denarii see **Money**; for sextarius see **Weights and measures**)

49

Doctors and medicine

Doctors were introduced into Italy from **Greece** and they were mostly men. There were also some specialists, such as those who treated eye complaints. Many doctors were freed **slaves** – freedmen. Towns could employ doctors for the community and pay them a small salary. However, there was no proper training for doctors and no official registration either, so anyone could declare himself a doctor.

The Romans worshipped a **god** of healing called Aesculapius, but there were also many practical treatments for illness and injury. For example, hot mashed turnips were considered to be a cure for chilblains and mustard was used for stomach upsets. Pharmacists sold prepared treatments, such as eye ointments.

Doctors were able to treat some very serious illnesses and they had a wide range of instruments for surgery. Roman doctors could cut into the skull to relieve pressure on

This stone stamp was used to mark sticks of eye ointment. The letters are reversed so that they could be read on the ointment. The words give the eye doctor's name, Titus Vindacius Ariovistus.

This is one of the best-preserved sets of doctors' instruments ever found. It comes from Italy and was made in the 1st or 2nd century AD. The set contains drug boxes, scalpel handles, forceps, probes, needles, catheters and bone chisels.

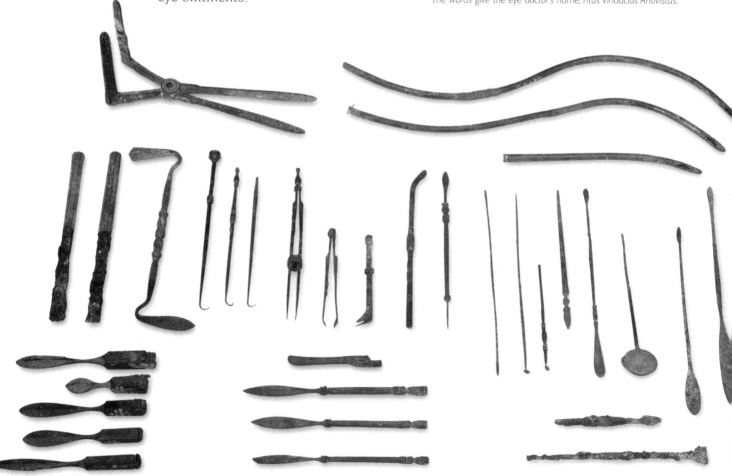

the brain, and they were able to make false teeth and even artificial limbs. Nevertheless many people doubted the ability of doctors to cure the sick – one writer, **Martial**, wrote sarcastically of a doctor he knew: 'Until recently, Diaulus was a doctor, now he's an undertaker. He is still doing, as an undertaker, what he used to do as a doctor.'

Druids

The Druids were the priests of the religion practised by the Celtic peoples. The Romans had trouble with the Druids, in particular those in **Gaul** and in **Britain**.

The Druids were an important and a special class of people in the Celtic world. They had privileges and acted as teachers and judges as well as priests. They had their own Chief Druid and held an assembly each year.

Our knowledge of these Celtic priests is not particularly good, however, and much of what we do know comes from the writings of **Julius Caesar**. The Romans believed that the Druids helped to stir up resistance to their occupation and rule. As a result they outlawed them and tried to wipe them out, along with their religion, during the **invasion** and occupation of Britain.

Right: These human remains from the 1st century AD are from Lindow Moss bog in Britain. The man was given some special bread and a drink containing mistletoe before his skull was smashed. He was then strangled with a cord and his throat was cut before he was put in the bog. Some archaeologists think that this was perhaps a sacrifice made by the Druids.

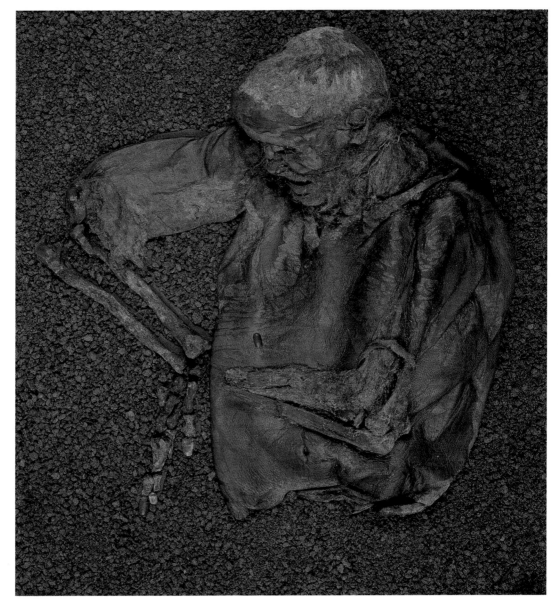

E

Eastern empire

In AD 284 the emperor **Diocletian** changed the way the Roman **empire** was governed. He ruled the eastern part from the city of Nicomedia in Bithynia while his colleague Maximian ruled the western part from **Rome**. The Roman empire returned to being ruled by just one **emperor** under **Constantine** in AD 324, but the capital was at **Constantinople** (now Istanbul in Turkey) from AD 330. There was another change in AD 395 when the emperor Theodosius divided the empire into western and eastern parts, with capitals at both Rome and Constantinople. The western part of the empire fell victim to increasing attacks from **barbarian** tribes and the last Roman emperor in the west, who was called Romulus Augustulus, reigned only for a short time, from AD 475 to 476. After that, the Roman empire survived only in the east, as the Byzantine empire.

Below: A plate and drinking vessel.

Eating out

Many people living in **apartments** had no means of cooking for themselves and went out for snacks or ready-made dishes to bring home. All towns had hot-food bars, called *thermopolia*. They were easy to spot because large containers were set into a counter that faced the street.

In **shops** the containers might hold **wine**, fish sauce, **olives or olive oil**. Paintings on the walls indicated what was on the menu at

Above: Two metal frying pans – the one on the left may have been used for cooking bread rolls or poaching eggs.

Right: The remains of a hot-food bar in Herculaneum, the Roman city, which, along with Pompeii, was destroyed when Mount Vesuvius erupted in AD 79.

each particular establishment. At **Ostia** one snack bar sold green olives, turnips, eggs, cheese and watermelon. You could drink hot, sweet-spiced wine or honey water. In the hot-food bars, a fire burned under the counter to keep the **food** hot, or at least warm.

Egypt

Egypt had been conquered by the Greek King Alexander the Great of Macedonia (in **Greece**) in 330 BC and he founded the city of **Alexandria** there. After his death a Macedonian general called Ptolemy established himself as king. After him, all Egyptian kings were called Ptolemy. The Romans began to be interested in Egypt in the 2nd century BC. By the 1st century BC a Ptolemy was on the throne only because the Romans allowed it. When the Ptolemy who was nicknamed Auletes (the 'flute-player') died, his will named his daughter **Cleopatra** and his son Ptolemy joint rulers but with Rome as their guardians. In 30 BC the emperor **Augustus** 'added Egypt to the **empire** of the Roman people', as he wrote. Augustus kept the **province** of Egypt to himself and ruled it through his own chosen officials. Egypt was very important to the Romans, since it was from here that vast quantities of grain from its fertile land were brought to **Rome** to feed the 200,000 Romans who were registered for free **food**. The Roman **emperor** was represented as a pharaoh in Egypt.

Emperor

A Roman emperor was the supreme ruler of the **empire** with all the power and authority of a king. The title emperor comes from the **Latin** word *imperator*, meaning an army commander who has won a great victory and been awarded a **triumph**. Octavian (later called **Augustus**) was the first ruler to adopt the title of emperor to emphasize his military authority after the **civil war**. (See the list of emperors on pages 154–5.)

This coin depicting the emperor Otho indicates the many powers of an emperor. The abbreviated words explain his titles: IMP for 'Imperator'; CAES for Caesar and AVG for 'Augustus', which were used as words for emperor; PM for 'Pontifex Maximus', the chief priest; and COS for 'Consul'.

Empire

After the assassination of **Julius Caesar**, his adopted son, Octavian, eventually defeated all his enemies and became the most powerful man in **Rome**. In 27 BC he was given the special title **Augustus**, meaning 'a person to be respected'. He took many titles for himself, including *imperator*, which meant an **army** commander who had won a great victory. It came to mean **emperor**. Augustus became emperor of Rome and, although he talked about restoring the democratic **republic**, he never did. Rome was now an imperial state – the Roman **empire**.

Ephesus

Attalus III, king of Pergamum, left his kingdom to the Romans in his will. When Attalus died, in 133 BC, the city of Ephesus (on the coast of modern Turkey) became the capital of the new Roman **province** of **Asia**. Ephesus had been an important and a wealthy city in ancient **Greek** times and was famous for its **temple** to the Greek **goddess** Artemis (see **Diana**). The temple was one of the Seven Wonders of the Ancient World. The Romans added many new public **buildings**, including a library. The **Christian** St Paul visited Ephesus and caused a riot by upsetting the city's silversmiths, who sold offerings to the worshippers of Artemis.

Equites

Romans were divided into three classes: **plebeians**, equites and **patricians**. The equites (which means 'knights') were citizens whose property was valued by the censor to be at least 400,000

Ephesus: a view of the theatre and the colonnaded street leading to the baths and what was once the city's harbour.

sesterces (see **Money**). The **emperors** chose **officials** such as procurators and **army** officers such as tribunes from the class of equites.

Etruscans

North of **Rome** was an area known as Etruria – the land of the Etruscans. By the 7th century BC these people had formed themselves into twelve states. They had become wealthy and powerful through agriculture and trading metal with the **Greeks** and other peoples. They had also developed industries, such as **metal working** and **pottery**. They built large **cities**, which were laid out with **roads** and water and sewage systems (see **Lavatories and sewers** and **Water supply**).

Although the Romans claimed that their country was founded by warrior heroes descended from the **gods**, many things we associate with the Romans were, in fact, invented by the Etruscans. For example, they developed a system to bring water into their cities using **aqueducts**.

We know quite a lot about the Etruscans from the remains that have survived, especially their richly decorated underground tombs. Inscriptions in the Etruscan language have also been found.

Left: The Etruscans were skilled metalworkers, especially with bronze. The back of this polished mirror has an engraving of people playing a board game that the Romans called 'duodecim scripta', meaning Twelve Lines (see page 132).

Left: Games were an important part of Etruscan life. This beautiful little figurine, which is made of bronze, shows a woman athlete running. Etruscan athletes also competed in the long jump.

F

'In the vast estates in Gaul a very large machine called a vallus with teeth at the edge and carried on two wheels is driven through the corn.'
Pliny the Elder

These Roman farm tools have reconstructed wooden handles. From left to right they are: an iron scythe for cutting grain; a rake with iron prongs; a turf cutter; a solid iron peg, called a 'mower's anvil', for supporting the scythe while it was being sharpened; and a rake made from the antler of red deer.

Family

Although the English word 'family' comes from the **Latin** *familia*, it does not quite have the same meaning. In Latin the word meant family in the sense of parents, **children**, relatives and all the other people and possessions within the house. In fact, 'household' might be a better translation for *familia*.

The law gave the man complete authority over his 'family' – for example, he owned his wife, children and slaves as well as the furniture. As head of the family, the man acted as the family **priest** and made **sacrifices** and offerings to the **household gods**.

Farming tools

The farm manager (see **Farms**) had to make sure that the tools and **machinery** to keep the farm operating were in good repair. Most of this work would be done on the farm itself – the farm labourers carrying out small repairs while specialist workers, such as blacksmiths (see **Metal working**), were brought in for major jobs or annual maintenance.

Farms needed a variety of different hand tools – for example, axes, hooks and scythes for cutting trees and harvesting crops, as well as spades, shovels, saws, hoes, rakes and hammers. They also needed ploughs to break up the soil. Some Roman farmers used a harvesting machine called a *vallus*. A **sculpture** of one was found in the **province** of Gallia Belgica at Buzenol, now in Luxembourg. The *vallus* was pushed by a donkey or oxen and cut the crops down with a sharp blade.

Farms

To a Roman the word **villa** might mean a holiday house or a working farm, even a large country estate. Many Romans acquired large amounts of land in territory conquered or occupied by the **army** and made into **provinces**. Many native farmers who held small amounts of farm land were forced out by the new wealthy landowners. They usually ended up unemployed in cities such as **Rome** (see **Gracchi**). When a *colonia*, or colony, was established (see **Cities and new towns**), the ex-soldiers, who became the first inhabitants, were given some of the surrounding land to farm.

Many villas have been excavated by archaeologists in different parts of the Roman **empire** and the fields investigated. Large farms were more important to the economy in the northern parts of the empire (**Britain**, **Gaul** and **Germany**, for example) than in the Mediterranean region. The heavy soil of the north was suitable for large-scale agriculture, and this could make the villa farmers very rich.

Many small Roman farms had a simple farmhouse for the family and outbuildings for workers, who were usually **slaves**. But there were large farming estates. On these, the buildings were also larger and usually grander, as the writer **Columella** tells us: 'A farm should be in a place with a healthy climate, with fertile soil, with some flat ground and some hilly, on an eastern or southern slope – but not too steep. The villa should have three sections: the "villa urbana" – the house of the owner, the "villa rustica" – the house of the farm manager and labourers, and the "villa fructuaria" – the storehouses'.

Farms had a number of labourers to do the work in the fields, take care of the animals, or prepare produce (such as pressing **olives** into oil) for sale. Life for most of them was hard, and slave labourers who tried to escape or who caused trouble were usually chained together, even while they were working.

In charge of the farm labourers was the farm manager, called the *vilicus*. He might be a slave himself. Columella says that the *vilicus* 'must be someone who has been hardened by farm-work since childhood and tested by practical experience'. Another writer, Marcus Cato, says that he: 'must not be an idler, he must always be sober. He must be the first to rise in the morning and the last to bed. Before that he must see that the farm is shut up and that everyone is asleep in the right place and that the animals have fodder'.

A large farmhouse also needed slaves to keep it in order, even when the owner and the family were not there. The housekeeper, called the *vilica*, was in charge of the household slaves. She may also have been a slave and may have been the wife of the farm manager. Cato says of her that: 'She must be clean herself and keep the farm clean and neat. She must clean and tidy the fireplace every night before she goes to bed'.

This bronze statuette, which was found in Britain, shows a ploughman at work with his team of oxen. The team has a bull (the larger animal) and a cow, which, because they were different in size and strength, would have been quite difficult to control. This statuette might show a special custom of marking the boundary of a field with a male and a female animal.

A bronze jug with an elaborately decorated handle. This fine piece would have been used only for the table, perhaps to hold wine.

Food

The Romans ate a lot of the same things we do today, including vegetables, fruit, meat and fish, but because these ingredients were used, to our way of thinking, in unusual combinations, their food did not really taste like most of the **meals** we would now recognize.

We know quite a lot about Roman food from writers of the time, especially **Apicius**. Roman recipes contained many ingredients that were used as food flavourings. They used lots of herbs, such as coriander, oregano, mint, thyme, fennel, sage, thyme and mint, for example. They also imported (see **Import/export**) spices from the eastern parts

This mosaic, which was made for a house near Rome in about AD 100, shows a variety of sea creatures – fishes, an eel, an octopus and a lobster – that would have been part of the Roman diet.

Cabbages with leeks

Put boiled cabbages into a shallow saucepan and season with liquamen, oil, ordinary wine and cumin. Sprinkle with pepper, leeks, caraway seeds and fresh coriander.

Apicius

of their **empire** and from countries further away, such as India. The most important spice for a Roman cook was pepper, but recipes also demanded nutmeg, cloves, cardamom and ginger, for example (see **Food supply**).

Roman cooks also used prepared sauces that they could buy in bulk. The favourite was one called *liquamen*, made from salted fish and fish guts that had been left out in the sun to become liquid. It was transported to **shops** and markets in large pottery vessels called **amphorae**.

Foreign gods

The Romans accepted **gods and goddesses** into their religion who were worshipped in the countries they conquered and ruled. For example, in **Britain** they came across the worship of the goddess Sul (associated with the sun and water) and linked her with their own goddess **Minerva**. Worship of the gods **Mithras** from Persia, and Isis and Serapis from **Egypt** was imported into **Rome** and across the **empire**. But some religions, such as those practised by **Christians** and **Druids**, were outlawed.

Above: This is the Roman equivalent of a food blender. It is called a 'mortarium' and was used for grinding food, spices and herbs. The bowl has a lip for pouring, and inside there are little pieces of grit set into the fired clay. Roman cooks used a pestle to squash the ingredients on to the rough surface. This particular piece of kitchen equipment was made by a potter called Sollus who stamped his name on the rim.

These fine-quality Roman pots, pans and dinnerware were imported across the English Channel into Britain just before the Roman conquest by the emperor Claudius. Here you can see flagons for holding wine, large dinner plates, bowls, cups and even a metal frying pan.

59

Below: An artist's impression of a Roman fort on Hadrian's Wall. This fort guarded the eastern end of this frontier at Wallsend in Britain. It was built of stone with barracks for the infantry and cavalry. In the centre was the commander's house, headquarters building, a granary and a hospital.

Forts

The size of an **army** fort depended on the size of the army unit based there. Some forts were enormous and could house an entire **legion** of between 5,000 and 6,000 men. Forts were laid out in a very regular fashion with streets between the buildings to give easy and fast access to the surrounding ramparts and walls. On each wall there was a defended gate.

Inside the fort was a range of buildings: the headquarters building for the commander-in-chief, his officers and the administration; **barracks** for the soldiers and stables for the horses if it were a **cavalry** unit; and other buildings such as granaries, storehouses, cookhouses, **lavatories**, a hospital, a house for the commander to live in and perhaps even a bath-house (see **Baths**).

Outside the walls of a permanent fort a civilian **settlement** usually grew up

Above: The reconstructed main gate of the fort at Saalburg near Frankfurt, Germany. The towers on each side extend out from the gates so that soldiers could fire down on any attackers.

with **shops** and taverns. Roman soldiers were not supposed to get married, but many did and their families often lived in these settlements close to the fort.

Forum

The main public **buildings** in any Roman town or city would be grouped around an area known as the forum. It was originally just an open space where markets could be held. In large cities the forum became so important for holding religious ceremonies and public meetings that markets were usually held elsewhere. The forum was also a place to meet to conduct business or politics.

In the open area of the forum you would expect to see a number of **statues** and busts of **gods and goddesses**, **emperors** and important local people.

'In the forum both public and private business is controlled by the town's officials. The site of the basilica should be fixed next to the forum in as warm an area as possible so that in winter businessmen may meet there without being troubled by the weather.'
The architect Vitruvius

An artist's impression of the forum at the city of Wroxeter in Roman Britain. The long building at the back of the open market place is a basilica.

Gauls

Celtic tribes called the Galli – the Gauls – came across the Alps in about 400 BC to look for new lands in Italy. One Roman historian, Polybius, said that they 'spent their time in war or in **farming** and that their only possessions were cattle and gold because this is what they could carry about with them'. In Italy they roamed the countryside in bands searching for loot.

In 390 BC the Gauls became a real threat to **Rome** itself. Most of the inhabitants fled while the Gauls besieged one of the high points of the city – the Capitoline Hill. The Gauls tried to reach the top of the hill at night. Those Romans who stayed were fast asleep. The historian **Livy** tells the story: 'One by one the Gauls pulled themselves up the side of the hill and reached the top. They were so silent that not even the guard dogs were woken up … but the Gauls could not escape the notice of the geese, which were sacred to the goddess **Juno**. These geese saved the Romans by the cackling and flapping of their wings.'

However, the Gauls were not easily overcome and finally the Romans paid them a large sum of gold to leave Italy. But Gaul, one of the Celtic territories incorporating modern-day France, Belgium, and parts of Germany and the Netherlands, was a rich country and the Romans were determined to bring it under their control.

Julius Caesar conquered large parts of Gaul in his campaigns of 58–51 BC and the new **provinces** were called Gallia – Gaul. The emperor **Augustus** began to establish **settlements** there. Many of the remains of major Roman towns, such as Arles, **Nîmes** and Orange, can still be seen today.

This gold coin was made in the 2nd century BC in Gaul. The design of these pre-Roman coins was taken from Greek coins of King Philip of Macedon who died in 336 BC.

'Nearly all the Gauls are tall, fair-haired and have a ruddy complexion. They are always quarrelling and are a proud and insolent people.'
Ammianus Marcellinus, a Roman soldier and historian writing in the 4th century AD

Germany

The people who became known as the Germani began to affect the Roman world in the 3rd century BC. They crossed the River Rhine in large numbers. **Julius Caesar** came across them in his campaigns in **Gaul**. The emperor **Augustus** wanted to expand into their territory but after three complete **legions** were wiped out by them in AD 9, there was a change of plan. There were military units based in Germania but it was not until the reign of the emperor Domitian, in about AD 90, that the territory of the Germani was organized into two **provinces** – Lower Germany and Upper Germany. There were many prosperous towns there, such as **Trier** and Cologne, which was known in other parts of the **empire** for its fine **pottery** and **jewellery**.

Gladiators

The fighters who battled each other in the **amphitheatres** were called gladiators, from the word *gladius* meaning 'sword'. But there were different sorts of gladiators. Some were heavily armed, with a helmet, arm and leg armour, and carried a sword and shield, like the statuette opposite. There were also

Gladiatorial and hunting scenes were popular decorative themes and they were often found on Roman mosaics. This one is in a house in Italica in Spain.

Left: Roman oil lamps often have scenes on them. This one, from the 1st century AD and found in London, shows two gladiators fighting.

Right: This carved bone statuette was found in Colchester in Britain. It shows a gladiator holding a sword and shield and wearing a protective helmet, similar in design to the one below.

lightly armed gladiators called *retiarii*, who carried a net and a three-pronged spear. A gladiator called a *secutor* usually fought a *retiarius*, and was armed with a soldier's sword and wore an arm-guard. Others (called *venatores*) also had to hunt and fight various wild **animals**.

Rich people and politicians (to gain favour with voters) paid for the training of gladiators. Gladiators were usually **slaves** or war prisoners. If they fought well, the organizer of games might free them.

The British Museum in London houses a carved relief that depicts two female gladiators. The relief is inscribed with a single word which translates as 'they were freed'. It is the only piece of evidence suggesting that female gladiators might have existed.

The grille over the face of this bronze helmet and the broad rim gave protection from blows from a sword. At the front is a bust of the god Hercules.

At lunchtime in the amphitheatre there was usually a chance to watch convicted criminals fight to the death. The last one left alive was brought back the next day.

'I happened to call in at a midday show in the amphitheatre, expecting some sport, fun and relaxation. It was just the opposite. By comparison the fights that had already taken place were merciful. Now they really get down to business – it's sheer murder. In the morning men are thrown to the lions or bears – at noon they are thrown to the spectators.
Seneca

63

Glass

This beautiful and very delicately made glass flagon was probably used for wine.

Although people made objects out of glass thousands of years before Roman times, it was the Romans who made it an industry by inventing glass-blowing. Glass-workers used a long iron tube to blow air into a lump of molten glass. In this way, large numbers of glass objects could be mass-produced. A few Roman **houses**, and other buildings, also had window glass, although it could not made in large panes.

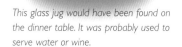

This glass jug would have been found on the dinner table. It was probably used to serve water or wine.

This robust square bottle may have been placed in a tomb.

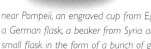

The Romans used a variety of glass vessels for food or drink, some from the provinces. From left to right they are: a blue jar from near Pompeii, an engraved cup from Egypt, a German flask, a beaker from Syria and a small flask in the form of a bunch of grapes.

64

Gods and goddesses

The early Romans believed that powerful spirits, which they called *numina*, were everywhere and controlled what humans did. Religion was an important part of everyone's life. **Gods** and spirits might be friendly if prayers were uttered or offerings given. This could happen in **temples** or at roadside or household altars (see **Household gods and shrines**) or any other places considered sacred. In time, the Romans adopted gods and goddesses from other peoples, especially from the **Etruscans** and the **Greeks** and, as they grew more powerful, from the further parts of the **empire** (see **Foreign gods**). **Emperors** were also worshipped as gods – the emperor **Claudius**, for example, had a temple built after his death for his worship in **Colchester** in the **province** of **Britain**. The Romans portrayed their gods and goddesses as larger than life-size human beings in **wall paintings** and **statues**.

The best-known Roman gods today are the family of gods known as the Olympians. These were Greek gods who were thought to live on Mount Olympus in **Greece**, but when the Romans adopted them they changed their names – for example the king of the gods, called Zeus in Greece, became **Jupiter** in Rome.

Gods and goddesses were thought to have power over a number of things and so they are often recorded with two names: the god **Mars** was the protector of cattle as Mars Silvanus and **Apollo** Sminthius was the guardian of farmers against mice.

This head of the god Mercury was originally part of a larger statue found in a temple in the province of Britain.

On the left is Mercury, the god of merchants, who, with his winged hat, also carried messages for the gods. On the right is Mars, the god of war.

A coin of the emperor Theodahad, the last Ostrogothic ruler of Italy before the reconquest of the west by the emperor Justinian. Theodahad is wearing the typical helmet-like crown of an Ostrogoth king. The reverse side shows Victory. The coin may have been minted in Rome in AD 536.

'A report spread that the Goths had suddenly descended like a whirlwind from the high mountains and were ravaging and destroying everything in their path.'
Ammianus Marcellinus, writing in the 4th century AD

Goths

The Goths were a German tribe who left their original home in Sweden and moved south, eventually settling in southwest Russia in the 3rd century AD. In the AD 260s they began to raid the Roman **empire**, first **Greece** and **Asia** and the **provinces** around the River Danube. The Romans called those who lived around the Black Sea Goths, but there were two distinct groups – the eastern group called the Ostrogoths and the western group called the Visigoths (see **Barbarians**). By the 4th century they were being hard pressed by the Huns, and the Visigoths moved into Italy. Under their leader, Alaric, they sacked **Rome** itself in AD 410. The Ostrogoths, under their leader Theoderic, moved west in the later 5th century and conquered Italy, making their capital at Ravenna.

Gracchi

As the Roman state expanded after the wars of the 3rd and 2nd centuries BC, including those against **Carthage**, land was given to rich owners, who then formed large farming estates (see **Farms**). Poor farmers often had to give up their smallholdings and settle in **Rome**. Usually unemployed, these farmers had to be fed by the government. When Tiberius Gracchus was appointed an **official**, called a tribune, to look after the interests of the **plebeians** in 133 BC, he proposed a law that would give much of the new land acquired by Rome to farmers in small plots. The farmers then paid a rent to the state.

The law was passed, but there was fierce opposition from wealthy Romans who stood to lose their large estates, and they had Gracchus murdered. His brother Gaius Gracchus (the two are known as the Gracchi) took up the challenge when he was elected tribune in 124 BC. He sponsored a number of laws in the **senate** that helped the poor. When he tried to be elected for the third time he was hunted down. To avoid capture he had a **slave** stab him to death, but 3,000 of his followers were arrested and executed.

Greece

The Romans admired ancient Greek culture, language and literature and finally included Greece as part of the Roman **empire**. The Romans divided Greece into three **provinces** with a governor in charge of each – Macedonia, Epirus and Achaea. The Achaeans tried to fight against Rome in the 2nd century BC but the Romans defeated them and completely destroyed one of their main towns, **Corinth**. **Julius Caesar** established a new town here as a *colonia*, or colony, for retired soldiers. The emperor **Hadrian** visited the ancient capital, **Athens**, and by the end of his reign had transformed the city.

Greeks

The Romans admired the Greeks and Greek culture. Educated Romans spoke the (now ancient) Greek language.

There were historical connections between **Greece** and **Rome**. From about 750 BC the Greeks established a number of colonies in southern Italy, Sicily and southern France. The Romans finally

These are the remains of the main street in the city of Dion in northern Greece. The Greek city was rebuilt by the Roman consul Philippus after he had captured it. The ruts in the stone surface of this street were caused by the wheels of carts.

'I prefer that a boy should learn Greek as his first language. He will soon pick up Latin, whether he likes it or not, as it is in general use.'
Quintilian, the first Roman university professor in Athens

occupied all these territories. The Romans also fought a successful campaign against an **invasion** by King Pyrrhus from Epirus in Greece in 280 BC. Later, the Romans took over the entire Greek mainland and incorporated it into the **empire**.

Gymnasium

Attached to or located close to public **baths** you would commonly find a gymnasium (from the **Greek** word *gymne*, meaning nude). The gymnasium was an open exercise ground surrounded by a colonnaded walkway. Here, bathers could exercise, wrestle, run and perform gymnastics. A school of gymnastics was often associated with a gymnasium.

The idea came from ancient **Greece**, and university-style teaching was common in the shady colonnades of a gymnasium. The tradition continued into Roman times, especially in **Athens** and other Greek **cities**.

67

Hadrian

Hadrian is famous today for the great wall he built across northern **Britain** as a frontier defence for the **province** of Britain, now known as **Hadrian's Wall**. He was one of **Rome**'s greatest **emperors** and increased the **empire** to its largest extent in the 2nd century AD. Hadrian reigned over a peaceful empire for twenty years.

Hadrian was born in Rome but his family moved to **Italica** in Spain (**Hispania**), where they had originally come from. When his father died, the ten-year-old Hadrian became the ward of the future emperor **Trajan**, who also came from Italica. He held public office and served in the **army**. The emperor Trajan and Hadrian were good friends, and he had the support of Plotina, the emperor's wife.

Hadrian was serving as the governor of **Syria** when news reached him of Trajan's death. The empress Plotina held back the news to ensure that Hadrian would succeed to become head of state. It was said that she even forged certain documents confirming Trajan's adoption of Hadrian as his heir.

Hadrian loved the culture and literature of ancient **Greece**. He was the most travelled of all the Roman emperors and visited the city of **Athens** three times. He also restored many of its ancient buildings. He was the first emperor to wear a full beard, which was a Greek fashion. He was also known as a builder in Rome. He built for himself a vast and grand palace at Tivoli, 24 km (15 miles) outside of Rome. He rebuilt Rome's **temple** to all the **gods**, the **Pantheon**, as well as a huge, circular mausoleum to be buried in. Hadrian died in AD 138.

A statue of the emperor Hadrian, found in a sanctuary to the god Apollo. In his left hand is an offering of laurel to the god.

Hadrian created buildings in his palace at Tivoli, outside Rome, to remind him of his travels through the empire. He had seen a canal near Alexandria in Egypt and created these arches, columns and statues decorating the edge of an ornamental lake.

Hadrian's Wall

The Romans used natural boundaries (mountains or seas) as the frontiers for their **provinces** and their **empire** wherever they could. A line of fortified banks and ditches and permanent **forts** formed the northern defence line, known as the *limes*, between the River Rhine and the River Danube.

In **Britain** the Romans used a similar solution. Following their **invasion** of AD 43 the Romans occupied most of the **province** of Britain but gave up the attempt to conquer Scotland and withdrew, shortly after AD 100, to a patrolled frontier road, known as the Stanegate. This road ran across one of the narrowest parts of the country, from the River Tyne to the River Solway. In AD 117 there seems to have been unrest among the British tribes, and when the emperor **Hadrian** visited Britain in AD 121/122 he decided to strengthen this frontier line. He ordered a great stone wall to be built, about 3.25 km (2 miles) north of the Stanegate.

The wall stretched eighty Roman miles (117 km/73 miles), was 6.5 m (21 ft) high and 3 m (10 ft) thick with a defensive ditch outside 10 m (33 ft) wide and 3 m (10 ft) deep. But it was not just a wall that the three **legions** chosen to do the work had to complete. Small forts, known as milecastles, were built on to the wall at intervals of a

Part of Hadrian's Wall looking west towards the fort of Housesteads in Britain.

Roman mile (1.5 km) to provide accommodation for between eight and thirty-two soldiers who patrolled the wall. These milecastles were the only entrances through the wall for the native people and they provided a convenient point to levy tax on goods passing through and to control the movement of people across the frontier. Between each milecastle were two evenly spaced lookout turrets with enough room to accommodate twelve men.

There were also sixteen forts to provide permanent housing for the **army** based on Hadrian's Wall, outpost forts beyond the wall, signal beacons and a broad, flat-bottomed ditch, called the *vallum*, which provided protection from attack from south of the wall, within the province. Many different soldiers served on the wall from countries including those now known as Iraq, Turkey, Belgium, **Germany**, Croatia, France and Morocco.

Later, other attempts were made to conquer Scotland and a new frontier defence, this time a turf wall, was ordered by Hadrian's successor, the emperor Antoninus Pius, 160 km (100 miles) north of Hadrian's Wall. It required up to twenty-six forts to make the frontier effective, and in about AD 158 it was abandoned in favour of Hadrian's Wall. This wall remained the northernmost frontier of Britain for most of the Roman period.

Hairstyles

Roman men and women took a great deal of trouble over the way their hair looked, and particular styles were popular at various times. This is also true today, but in Roman times fashion seems to have changed more slowly. A fashionable hairstyle for a woman, for example, might last for twenty years.

Although some hairstyles for women were simple, others were very elaborate and required a **slave** to plait and arrange the hair using pins or even a thin hairnet called a *reticulum*, heated curling tongs and hair oil. Women dyed their hair – blonde and red were favourite colours. Wigs, or hair pieces, often made with the hair of captured blonde women from **Germany**, or dark-haired women from India, were often used.

Most men were clean-shaven up to the 2nd century AD, at which point beards became popular. **Hadrian** was the first **emperor** to have a full beard. Hairstyles varied, too, from century to

This bust of a Roman lady was made around AD 150–160. Her hair is arranged in a bun high on her head.

This comb, which is carved from bone, was discovered in a grave. A woman's name, Modestina, and the word 'farewell' are carved between the comb's teeth.

The remains of the temple of Jupiter in Heliopolis, which is in modern-day Lebanon.

This little silver object is actually a pepper pot. It was buried in the 5th century AD and was found in eastern Britain. It depicts a lady, perhaps an empress, with an elaborate hairstyle and wearing a necklace and earrings.

century: from short hair combed forward to full curls to the crew-cut popular in the 3rd century AD. Men used hair oil and curling tongs. The poet **Martial** complained about one particular man, saying that his 'greasy hair can be smelled all over the **theatre** of Marcellus'.

Heliopolis (Baalbek)

Heliopolis, in modern Lebanon, was a **Greek** and Roman city built on the site of the ancient Baalbek. It was famous for its enormous **temple** to the **god Jupiter**-Ba'al – combining a Roman god with one worshipped by the Canaanites. It was a depot for collecting wild **animals**, such as tigers, lions, leopards and wild asses, for the shows in the **amphitheatres**. These animals were shipped to **Rome**, probably via the **port** of **Alexandria** in **Egypt**, as well as coastal towns in the eastern Mediterranean.

Hispania

Spain (Hispania) had a long history of settlements by different peoples, including the Phoenicians, **Greeks** and **Carthaginians**. The emperor **Augustus** conquered the whole country and divided it into three **provinces**. Roman Spain's oldest and most famous town was **Italica**, which was the birthplace of the emperor **Trajan** and the home of the emperor **Hadrian**.

Spain was a very wealthy province and exported (see **Import/export**) huge quantities of **olive oil**, **wine** and fish sauce to other parts of the **empire**. There were also large numbers of state-owned metal mines there.

Horace

Horace was the son of an ex-**slave** but became one of Rome's best-known poets and a friend of the poet **Virgil**. Through Horace's poems, called the *Odes*, we can find out about various aspects of life in the reign of the emperor **Augustus**.

Household gods and shrines

Families had their own god or gods whom they thought protected them. These household gods, called the *lares*, had their own shrines or altars inside the **houses**. (see **Gods and goddesses**).

Houses

Although there were variations in the types of Roman houses, built to suit the climate of the **province** they were in, we do know that owners expected particular rooms and services. Many houses have been excavated by archaeologists across the Roman **empire**. Some, such as those in **Pompeii and Herculaneum**, are very well preserved. You could only afford to live in a house, rather than an **apartment**, if you were rich enough. Roman town houses had to be large enough to accommodate the family and their household **slaves**.

This mosaic is from the front entrance of a house in Pompeii. The fierce dog on a chain has the Latin words 'cave canem' underneath, meaning 'beware of the dog'. It did not always mean that there was a guard dog inside (some mosaics show a ferocious bear) but it did mean that passers-by were not encouraged to come in.

There were few window openings in Roman houses, partly to keep them private and secure from robbers and partly because it was difficult to make large enough panes of glass. Light reached inside by an opening in the roof of the *atrium*, the partly covered courtyard. Some houses were large enough to have a small walled garden at the rear, which also provided light to downstairs rooms.

Visitors reached most town houses along a passageway from the street. The door would almost certainly be guarded by one of the household slaves, acting as the doorman. Some houses have a **mosaic** of a ferocious animal, such as a snarling dog, to warn off uninvited visitors. If the mosaic was of a dog, there might also be the words *cave canem* – 'beware of the dog'!

The passageway led to the *atrium*, which had in its centre a water-collecting basin called an *impluvium*. Houses often had mosaics and **sculpture** here. Rooms surrounded this partly open courtyard. Stairs would lead from here to the upper floor, if there was one. From the *atrium* a visitor would pass into the main living room, called the *tablinum*. This large room was not just the family's living room but where the owner would receive guests and visitors, perhaps on government business. The *tablinum* could be closed off by curtains or even sliding doors, and some have been discovered in Herculaneum (see **Pompeii and Herculaneum**).

If the house had a garden, it would be at the rear and probably surrounded by a *colonnade* – a covered walk with a sloping roof supported by columns. This area also held the shrine (the *lararium*) to the **household gods**, and the kitchen and

dining room, or *triclinium*. The *triclinium* took its name from the three (*tri-*) couches that diners would recline on while eating from low tables (see **Food**).

Only a few Roman buildings had glass in the windows. Many had wooden shutters (see page 111) or iron grilles, like this one from a house in Britain.

The 'atrium' of a house in Herculaneum. The large opening at the back of the room would have been closed off with curtains or wooden doors when necessary.

73

Right: This mosaic comes from a house in Utica, north Africa. It was made around AD 200 and shows a hunting and fishing scene in marshland. You can see the fishermen's net stretching from boat to boat.

Right: This scene of a dog chasing a stag is from the mosaic floor of the main room of a house at Hinton St Mary, in the province of Britain (see page 95 for the full mosaic).

'You will laugh, and well you may, when I tell you that I, that Pliny whom you know well, captured three wild boars, and very fine ones at that! You? You ask. Yes I did! And I did so without interrupting any of my lazy ways or my peace and quiet. I was sitting by the hunting nets. Instead of hunting spears, I had a stylus and waxed writing tablets.'
Pliny the Younger

Hunting and fishing

'Are you reading, fishing, hunting, or doing all three? Well, you can do all of them together on the shores of Lake Como.' **Pliny** the Younger wrote this of Lake Como, in northern Italy, in a letter to a friend. For the wealthy, hunting and fishing were pleasant pastimes. Hunting parties were popular at country **villas**. Sometimes the hunters chased the **animals** on foot or on horseback, and hunting dogs were also used. Hunters also used decoys, traps and bows and

arrows. Very often, though, they would sit by nets and servants would drive animals towards them. Many other Romans, who could not afford to go hunting, watched the 'sport' in **amphitheatres** where animals of all sorts, from lions to snakes, were driven into nets or snares and then killed. Poorer people in the country relied on hunting and fishing as an important source of food and these activities may well have provided their only meat.

Fishing was also a favourite sport, using nets or traps or rods and lines with hooks. Fishing with a 'fly' on a line was also popular – the 'fly' was made from small feathers to imitate the behaviour of real flies or other insects landing on the surface of the water. We know that some fishermen dragged a line with many baited hooks behind boats.

There were many people living around the Mediterranean region who earned their living by supplying fresh fish for markets in towns or cities or by producing the distinctive fish sauce that the Romans enjoyed so much as a food flavouring (see **Food**).

Hypocaust

The Romans used an ingenious way of heating some of the rooms in their **houses** and **villas** and in the public **baths**. It was called the *hypocaust*. A furnace outside the building drove hot air under the floors of the room. The floors were raised on piles of tiles or stones and the floors had to be thick enough so they could be walked on. The hot air would pass through box-tile flues in the walls and escape through vents built into the roof. The nearer the room was to the furnace, the hotter the room would become. Hot rooms in baths were those right next to the furnace.

The *hypocaust* seems to have been incorporated into the design of public baths from around 100 BC, but by the time of the architect **Vitruvius** it was a common feature of private houses, with living rooms heated in this way. He describes in detail how to build one and explains how the floor under the supporting columns should always slope back towards the furnace so that the hot air can rise and flow easily.

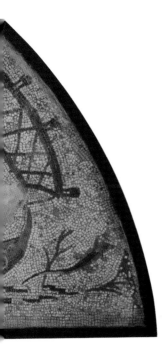

These public baths were built at the Roman town of Dion, in Greece. The tile floor of these baths is gone, but you can still see the little columns that supported it, creating the space that allowed the hot air of the hypocaust to heat the room.

Import/export

There were traders in all the **provinces** of the **empire** as well as in Italy and **Rome** itself and its **port**, **Ostia**. Provinces were known for their specialized goods. For example: from **Britain**, woollen cloaks, hunting dogs, silver and lead; from **Egypt**, papyrus and grain; from **Hispania**, **olive oil**, fish sauce, **wine** and cloth; from **Gaul**, wine and **pottery**; from **Greece**, wine, marble and purple dye; from north Africa, wild **animals** for the **amphitheatre**; from beyond the borders of the empire, silks, spices, perfumes and jewels.

A Roman **ship** was wrecked in the 4th century AD at Kenchreae, near

This is an advertisement for a firm of merchants at their offices in the port city of Ostia. The amphora between two palm trees shows that perhaps they imported oil or fish sauce from the eastern Mediterranean provinces.

Corinth in the province of Greece. Archaeologists were able to bring its cargo to the surface, and found wooden crates full of ready-made pieces for new buildings. Among them were wooden doors and a special type of marble flooring, called *opus sectile*, which was made in sections and laid on a backing of plaster, resin and pieces of broken **amphorae**.

The shipping merchants and ship-supply companies that had their offices in Ostia displayed the goods they carried and the places they journeyed to in **mosaics** in their chamber of commerce.

Invasion

The Romans sent their **armies** into most of the **provinces** they eventually took control of during the periods both of the **republic** and the **empire**. For example, the emperor **Trajan** invaded the country known as Dacia (now in modern Romania) because the Dacian king, Decebalus, was not honouring the terms of the peace treaty previously reached with **Rome**. Trajan invaded Dacia by crossing the River Danube with his troops and defeating the enemy in AD 101.

Britain was invaded three times by different Roman armies. **Julius Caesar** crossed from **Gaul** (now France) in 55 BC, and then in the following year 54 BC to try to stop the Britons from helping the resistance in Roman Gaul.

In his first invasion, using about 12,000 troops, Caesar forced the British tribes to accept his authority. He took a larger force, about 37,000 troops, on his second invasion. Caesar's forces were impressed with the skills of the British warriors on their chariots. He wrote that they: 'dash about all over the battlefield hurling their javelins. Then the warriors leap down from their chariots and fight on foot while their drivers take the chariots to the edge of the battle to wait for a signal to collect them.'

Caesar collected useful information about Britain and the British but he did not leave an occupying army there. In the autumn of AD 43, however, the emperor **Claudius** launched a full-scale invasion of Britain using a force of four **legions** (this was an army of about 40,000 people in total). His invading force even included some war elephants. These were probably intended to impress, or even scare, the native peoples.

The invading army turned into an occupying force, and eventually all of England and Wales became Roman.

Italica

The oldest Roman town in the **province** of **Hispania** (Spain) was Italica, near modern Seville. The town was founded by Scipio in 206 BC (see **Carthaginians and Hannibal**). The emperor **Trajan** was born here and the family of **Hadrian**, later to become **emperor**, moved here while he was still a child.

Italica was known to have a military club for teenagers, called a *collegium iuvenum*, and the young Hadrian was said to have carried out military training here at the age of fourteen. The emperor **Augustus** gave the town a charter to set up a town council (see **Cities and new towns**), but Hadrian made the town into a *colonia* and set about redesigning it and adding new public **buildings**. The town was doubled in size and laid out in regular blocks, or *insulae* (see **Cities and new towns**), with wide streets lined with colonnades. A huge **amphitheatre** was built to hold 25,000 spectators as well as a **theatre** and two public **baths**.

Italica was well known in **Rome** for the export of the best-quality **olive oil**, which was transported to the capital in enormous **amphorae**.

A number of extremely large private houses were built in the new colonia of Italica with fine mosaic floors and a range of rooms, including built-in lavatories.

Janus

Janus was the **god** of beginnings – Januarius, the first month of the year, was named after him. His name really means 'door' or 'gate'. Janus is pictured with two heads. His temple in the **forum** in **Rome** remained open in times of war, closed when there was peace. The doors were rarely closed.

Jerusalem

Jerusalem was the ancient capital of the Jewish king David, but it was turned into a splendid city in Roman times by King Herod the Great. His kingdom of Judaea was independent of the Romans until Herod's death in 4 BC. The Romans made Judaea a **province** and moved the capital to Caesarea. The emperor Titus destroyed Jerusalem during the Jewish Revolt of AD 66–70 (see **Vespasian** and **Masada**) and he stationed the 10th **legion** there. The emperor **Hadrian** resettled Jerusalem as a *colonia* (see **Cities and new towns**). Due to the city's association with Christ (see **Christianity**), it became a place of pilgrimage by the late 4th century AD.

Jewellery

We have evidence of Roman jewellery from a number of sources pictured in this book. First there are the remains of different sorts of jewellery, often excavated from burials. Then jewellery is sometimes portrayed on paintings, as you can see opposite, or on sculptures or on objects,

This gold body chain was buried at a time of trouble and unrest in 5th-century AD Britain. It fastens at the front in an oval setting of amethyst from Egypt and garnets. The empty settings probably contained pearls. At the back, the chains come together in another setting with a gold coin of the emperor Gratian.

such as the pepper pot on page 71. Jewellery, especially rings, provided an opportunity to show that the wearer supported a particular **emperor** or a **god** or **goddess**. For the same reason a coin was sometimes inserted into a piece of jewellery (see the body chain above).

Several different sorts of metal – silver, gold and bronze, as well as bone, glass and precious stones – were used to make jewellery. Skilled craftspeople hammered sheets of gold and cut out intricate shapes, twisted metal wire into woven necklaces or poured molten metal into moulds. There were rings for ears and for fingers and even keys to little boxes attached to finger rings. A ring was given to a new bride in the wedding ceremony, often showing two hands clasped together.

This elaborate piece of gold jewellery is a bracelet that came from Wales in the Roman province of Britain. Set into the gold are semi-precious gemstones called carnelian and blue glass. It was made for someone wealthy in the 1st or 2nd centuries AD.

This gold finger ring has a tiny portrait of Medusa, a terrible monster in Greek mythology.

A silver bracelet made in the 2nd century AD.

Left: In Roman Egypt some bodies were mummified (as the ancient Egyptians had done) and realistic portraits of the dead were placed over the head. This portrait of a wealthy woman is from around AD 100. It gives a good idea of the jewellery women wore at that time .

Below: This gold bracelet was buried along with the body chain shown opposite. There are letters around the bracelet that translate as 'Good luck to Lady Juliana'.

Josephus

The Roman historian Flavius Josephus was born Joseph ben (meaning 'son of') Matthias, a Jew who fought as a general in the revolt against **Rome** in AD 66–70. He was taken prisoner by the Romans and became an interpreter and adviser to Titus, whose father was the emperor **Vespasian**. Josephus was on friendly terms with the imperial family and was given Roman citizenship. Among his books is *The Jewish War*, an account of the Jewish revolt against Rome.

Julius Caesar

Julius Caesar claimed that he was descended from the **gods** through the Trojan prince **Aeneas**, the son of the **Greek** goddess Aphrodite (called **Venus** in Roman times).

Julius Caesar was probably born sometime between 102 and 100 BC into an important **patrician** family. He was related to **Marius**, a politician and an enemy of the dictator **Sulla** during the **civil war** of 83 BC. Caesar began his career in the **army**, serving in the eastern part of the **empire**. After his time in the army he went on to have a political career, taking various public offices (see **Officials**). He was elected to the highest office in the **republic**, that of **consul**, in 60 BC.

After his consulship Caesar went to govern the **provinces** of northern Italy and **Gaul**. He decided to launch a campaign against the Celtic peoples, not only in order to make existing Roman territory safe but also to increase its size and influence. Part of this campaign against the Celts was to invade **Britain**, in both 55 and 54 BC. His successful military campaigns made him popular among the soldiers and the people at home, but they also aroused jealousy and alarm among other important people in **Rome**. In 49 BC his rival, **Pompey**, persuaded the **senate** to order Caesar to disband his army. He refused and civil war broke out.

The war ended four years later when Caesar finally defeated Pompey's sons in Spain. Caesar was now the most powerful person in Rome and declared himself 'dictator for life'. Others feared that this was the end of the Roman republic, with people able to vote for their leaders. **Marcus Brutus**, Gaius Cassius and others plotted to kill Caesar and on 15 March 44 BC they stabbed him to death outside the senate house. His murder resulted in another civil war when his adopted son Octavian (later to be

'Before, members of the senate, we only had a route through Gaul. All the other territories were occupied by peoples who either were hostile to us or could not be trusted. Caesar has fought very successfully against the fiercest of peoples in great battles and made them part of the Roman state.'
Cicero

'He was a bit of a dandy. He always had his hair carefully trimmed and used to comb his few hairs forward to cover his baldness.'
Suetonius

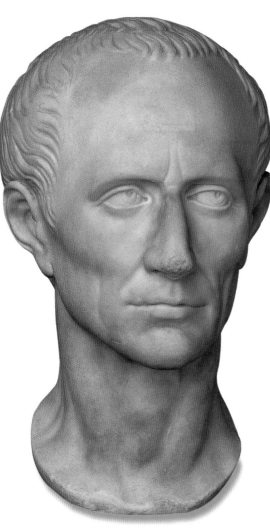

A finely carved marble head of the emperor Julius Caesar, the most powerful man in Rome until his murder in 44 BC.

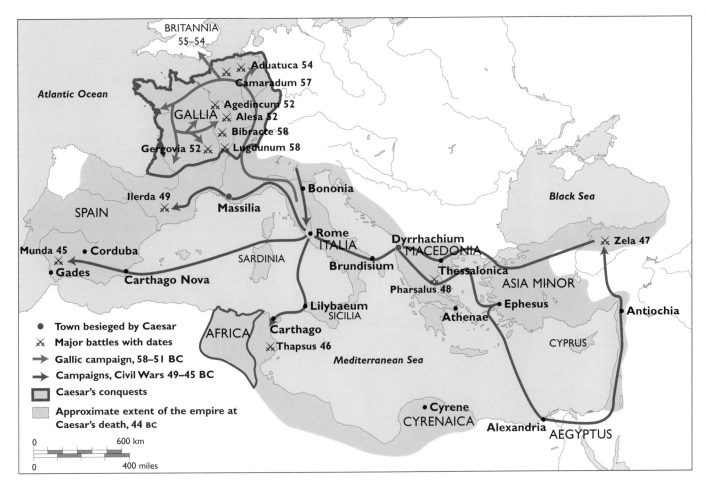

This map details the military career of Julius Caesar, showing Rome's domination of the Mediterranean region on his death in 44 BC.

known as the emperor **Augustus**) came back from **Greece**, where he had been studying, to avenge his father's death.

Juno

Juno was the supreme **goddess** of **women** and the wife of the king of the gods, **Jupiter**. Juno was thought to look after women in childbirth and newly born children. The most important festival in her honour, called the Matronalia, was held on the first day of March. Women would offer **sacrifices** to Juno on their birthdays. She was worshipped in **Rome** as the Queen of Heaven, alongside Jupiter and **Minerva**. The month of June, originally called Junonius, was considered to be the most favourable month for getting married (see **Weddings**).

This small bronze statuette of the goddess Juno was made in Rome sometime in the mid-1st century AD.

81

A bronze statuette of the god Jupiter.

Jupiter

The Romans called Jupiter 'the greatest and the best' and worshipped him as king of all their **gods**. He was the god of thunder and of the sky, and his symbols were a thunderbolt and an eagle. He was associated with war, the making of treaties and the swearing of oaths. He was thought to be able to punish those who broke their oaths by killing them with his thunderbolt. White was his sacred colour, and white **animals** were often **sacrificed** to him.

This gold coin of the emperor Justinian was minted in Constantinople. His Latin name – IVSTINIANVS – can be clearly seen.

Justinian

By the end of the 5th century AD, much of the western Roman **empire** had been taken over by invading peoples from the north and east. Justinian, who came to power in AD 527 as **emperor** of the eastern Roman empire, based in **Constantinople**, decided to reclaim the west. Justinian's wife, Theodora, was empress. He conquered north **Africa**, taking it back from the **Vandals** in AD 533. He went on to reconquer Italy from the Ostrogoths (see **Goths**) in his campaigns of AD 535–54 and he reoccupied southern Spain in AD 552. Justinian's general, Narses, was appointed his ruler in the west with his capital at Ravenna in northern Italy, formerly the capital of the Ostrogoth king Theodoric. Justinian built splendid **Christian** churches, including the magnificent Church of St Sophia in Constantinople. The church still survives, but it was converted into an Islamic mosque in 1453. After Justinian's death in AD 565 the reconquered lands were gradually lost again – the Lombards invaded Italy in AD 568 and by the late 7th century Africa and Spain were taken over by the Muslims.

This inscription is a good example of Latin letters carved in stone. It is a dedication to the god Apollo. Notice that our letter U is carved as a V, as on the coin shown opposite.

Latin

V

The 60 million people who lived in the Roman **empire** did not all speak the official language, Latin. But if you wanted to succeed in your career you had to learn it. The language is thought to have come to the area around **Rome** before the 8th century BC. It was the language of the people called the Latini, who lived in the plain of Latium near Rome (see **Writing**).

Lavatories and sewers

Most people had no lavatory in their **houses** or **apartments**. They made do with a chamber pot under the bed. There were public lavatories in towns, and **Rome** had 144. There were always lavatories in the public **baths**. Going to the lavatory was not a private affair as it is today. Some public lavatories had space for a hundred people. Men, **women** and **children** sat together on holes over a drain, along which water was constantly running (in baths it was the waste water). People used sponges attached to sticks as toilet paper.

The waste from public lavatories and private houses was carried away in underground sewers, often flushed by the water from the public baths. In Rome the largest sewer, called the Cloaca Maxima, carried waste and water into the River Tiber. The sewer was nearly 1 km (⅔ mile) long, and in places it was more than 4 m (13 ft) high and more than 3 m (10 ft) wide. Roman **forts** had their own lavatories for the troops to use.

L

'Dear host, I'm afraid I've wet my bed. "Why?" you ask. Well because there was no chamber pot in my room.'
Scratched on a wall in Pompeii

You can see below on the left the remains of a lavatory at the fort of Housesteads on Hadrian's Wall, in Britain. On the right is an artist's impression of what it probably looked like in Roman times.

Legions and legionaries

A legion (in **Latin** *legio*) was the main unit of the Roman **army**. By the 1st century AD a legion contained about 5,500 troops. To become a legionary soldier, a man had to be a Roman citizen and be recommended by someone. He served for 25 years and, on being discharged, he was given either a sum of money or land as a **farm**. A discharged soldier was known as a *veteranus*, or veteran.

A legionary's training was hard. He had to learn to fight, build a camp and, three times a month, march 30 km (18½ miles) in a day, with a fully loaded pack, weapons and armour.

Above: When a Roman soldier was discharged from the army a certificate, made in bronze, was given to him. This one belonged to a soldier called Reburrus, originally from Spain (the province of Hispania), but who had settled in Britain.

A statuette of a 2nd-century AD soldier wearing a tunic with a 'skirt' of leather straps and armour made from plates of iron.

Leptis Magna

This view is of the stage building of the theatre at Leptis Magna. The end wall of the stage is now missing but you can see what it looked like in the better-preserved example on page 107.

Leptis Magna, on the coast of the Roman **province** of **Africa**, had been a Carthaginian city. It became wealthy through trade with other parts of the **empire** and was well known for the **crops** of **olives** and wheat that grew around the city. The emperor Severus was born there

Above: A rare example of a Roman lighthouse, one of a pair to mark the entrance to Dover harbour in Britain. The site was later reused to build a castle, and a church was built next to this tower of tile and stone.

Left: This mosaic at Ostia shows a lighthouse with two merchant ships sailing by.

and revisited his birthplace in AD 203. To mark the occasion the townspeople erected a great memorial arch in his honour (see **Triumphs**) after he had provided the city with a new **forum**, **basilica** and harbour.

Lighthouses

Perhaps the earliest lighthouse was the famous Pharos at **Alexandria** and it was one of the Seven Wonders of the Ancient World. It was begun in the 3rd century BC. By the early 5th century AD we know that about thirty lighthouses stood in the Roman world, marking entrances to harbours. The stone or brick towers had fires in metal baskets on the top.

The writer **Suetonius** tells us that the emperor Caligula, in AD 40, visited Boulogne (in modern-day France) and ordered 'a tall lighthouse to be built, not unlike the one at Pharos, in which fires were to be kept going all night to guide ships'. Dover, an important British south-coast **port** in Roman times just as it is today, had two lighthouses to mark the entrance to its harbour. Remains of both are still there but one, in the grounds of Dover Castle, is particularly well preserved.

A marble head from Sicily portraying the Empress Livia as the goddess of corn, Ceres.

Livia

Livia was originally married to a **consul** called Tiberius, but he divorced her so she could marry Octavian (**Augustus)** in 38 BC, even though she had a son (Tiberius, who was named after his father and later became an **emperor**) and was pregnant at the time. The emperor Augustus loved her dearly and she had a strong influence on him throughout his reign. She worked hard, and in secret, to secure for her son Tiberius the position of emperor and was even suspected of poisoning Augustus.

After Augustus's death, when the **senate** declared him a **god**, she became his **priestess** and was known as Julia Augusta. Livia died in AD 29.

Livy

Titus Livius (referred to today as Livy) came from the town of Patavium (now Padua) in northern Italy. He was one of the most important Roman historians and wrote a history of **Rome**, *From the Founding of the City* as he called it, to 9 BC. His great historical work was published in 142 separate books.

London

Londinium (London) was an important **port** during the Roman **invasion** and became the capital of the **province** of **Britain** sometime after **Colchester** was badly damaged by a revolt in AD 60. It was in London where the governor of the **province** lived and conducted his affairs.

The Roman historian **Tacitus** mentions London as an important place for businessmen and trade. A **fort** for a permanent **army** unit was included inside the layout of the town, which became the largest in Roman Britain. A **temple** to the god **Mithras** was discovered and excavated inside the city's walls and the city's **forum** and **amphitheatre** have also been found.

This is the reverse side of a gold coin that celebrates the victories of the emperor Constantius over rebel emperors in Britain. He is shown on horseback near London (the abbreviation LON) and his title here is 'Restorer of Everlasting Light'.

Lucian

Lucian was a Greek writer who lived in the 2nd century AD and came from the **province** of **Syria**. He travelled as a teacher in **Greece** and Italy and held the post of government agent in charge of finances in part of the province of **Egypt**. He wrote satires as well as books on philosophy.

This model shows what the port of London may have looked like in
Roman times, with warehouses and a busy quayside.

M

This is a reconstruction of part of a huge waterwheel that was used to draw water from the mines at Rio Tinto in southern Spain in the 1st and 2nd centuries AD.

Machinery

The Romans used a number of machines to increase the efficiency of their work. They probably did not use wind power for mills, but they were the first to use water as a source of power for machinery. **Aqueducts** brought water to power wheels to turn the grindstones. An enormous complex of water-powered mills can still be seen today at Barbegal in southern France. Eight pairs of large wooden wheels, using a series of gears, drove the huge millstones. This was milling on an industrial scale for the 80,000 inhabitants of the Roman town Arelate (now Arles) in southern **Gaul** (modern-day France).

The Romans also used great wooden cranes to lift huge weights, such as stone blocks in building. The cranes were powered by wooden wheels turned by **slaves** walking inside. Wheels and gears were used in the **theatre** to lift **actors** on or off the stage from above or up through the stage floor. Similar devices lifted cages of wild **animals** up through the floor of some **amphitheatres**. To help with cutting the **crops** there was a machine called a *vallus*, which was pushed by a horse and cut the standing corn (see **Farming tools**).

Marching camps

For each night an **army** spent outside its permanent **fort**, on campaign or on manoeuvres, it built a temporary fort to protect itself. The ground was levelled and a rectangle marked out. The camp was measured out by engineers who travelled in advance of the main army. The soldiers dug a deep ditch and used the soil and turf to construct a high rampart topped with wooden stakes.

Inside the protected area of the camp the leather tents for the officers would be put up in the centre, with those for the ordinary soldiers arranged in straight lines around it. The engineers allowed for wide gaps between the lines of tents so that the soldiers could rush out to defend the ramparts.

This iron carpentry tool serves two purposes: first, its blunt end on the right acts as a hammer, while, second, the narrow, angled blade on the left of the tool is an adze, used to shape wood. Roman soldiers used tools like this to construct the wooden parts of their forts.

Marius

Marius was a general who won victories against the tribes who invaded Italy in the 2nd century BC. He was **consul** seven times. When **civil war** broke out with **Sulla** in the 1st century BC, Marius occupied **Rome** and murdered his enemies. Marius was responsible for creating a professional **army**.

Mark Antony

Marcus Antonius (now usually known as Mark Antony) was a general who fought with **Julius Caesar** in his campaigns in **Gaul**. He supported Caesar in his struggle with the **senate** in the **civil war**. Mark Antony delivered the funeral speech after Caesar had been murdered. He first fought as an ally of Octavian (later the emperor **Augustus**) and then helped to govern **Rome** with him. He became governor of the eastern **provinces** and met **Cleopatra** while he was at **Alexandria** in **Egypt**, and she had three children by him. War with Octavian followed his declaration that Cleopatra's son, Caesarion, by Julius Caesar, was the heir to Caesar, instead of Octavian. After Mark Antony's defeat by Octavian at Actium in 30 BC he committed suicide before his capture.

This silver coin depicting Mark Antony was minted at Ephesus, in modern-day Turkey, around 40 BC.

Mars

Mars was the **god** of war and was considered to be the most important god in **Rome** next to **Jupiter**. The priests of Mars danced in full armour in ceremonies. Mars was worshipped in festivals held in October and in March. Our month of March was originally named in honour of the god and it was called Martius by the Romans. Mars was also worshipped by farmers as the god who protected agriculture and cattle.

A statuette of the god Mars shown here wearing full body armour and, originally, carrying a weapon in his outstretched right hand.

Martial

Martial (his name in **Latin** was Martialis) was born and brought up in Spain (see **Hispania**) but spent thirty-five years in **Rome**. He wrote fifteen books of E*pigrams* in verse, containing about 1,500 poems. These short, witty poems give us details about all sorts of people and about daily life in Rome in the 1st century AD.

Martial tells us about the games in the **amphitheatre** (see his quote in **Colosseum** on page 42), and about life in the country (see **Villas**). But he is particularly witty about people he knows in Rome and the bustle on the streets. In one epigram he calls a man he knows, Caecilius, a 'buffoon' and accuses him of being like the 'pie-seller who shouts out as he carries around his warm pans of smoking sausages'.

Masada

During the reign of the emperor **Nero** the Jewish people in the **province** of Judaea rebelled against the imposition of Roman rule. The **emperor** sent an experienced and trusted general, **Vespasian**, to quell the rebellion. Vespasian had served on several major campaigns, including the **invasion** of **Britain** in AD 43 when he commanded the 2nd **legion**, 'Augusta'.

Nero appointed him governor of Judaea in AD 67 and he travelled there with three legions. The campaign went very well with major areas of resistance wiped out. Then in AD 68 Nero committed suicide. The next year Vespasian was proclaimed emperor by the legions in the east and he returned to **Rome** via **Alexandria**. He left the Jewish War in the hands of his son, Titus.

While his father was away, Titus captured the capital, **Jerusalem**, after a long **siege**. There were more than a million casualties and Jewish prisoners were said to have been slaughtered in

their hundreds in **amphitheatres** in **Syria** and in Rome.

Although Vespasian and Titus celebrated a triumph for the Jewish War in AD 71, the rebellion of the Jews was not yet over. A group of Sicarii (the word in **Latin** means 'bandit' or 'murderer') had taken over the fortress at Masada in AD 73 and continued to defy Roman rule. These people were Zealots – a band of Jews who fought for religious freedom and resisted Roman control of their land.

The fortress of Masada had been rebuilt by the Jewish king Herod with a private palace, strong walls and gates, storehouses and water reservoirs. It was also extremely well protected as it had been built on a natural rock hill.

The Romans besieged the fortress and built a wall all the way around the hill. On one side of the hill they built a great slope of earth and rocks to gain entrance to the fortress. Once at the top they constructed a great siege tower and battered the wall with catapults (**onagers**) and **battering rams**. Then in April AD 73 the Roman commander, Flavius Silva, broke through with his troops. The surviving Zealots, 960 in all, chose mass suicide rather than capture and execution by the Romans. Only one woman with her five children, who hid in a water cistern, were discovered still alive by the Romans.

The account of this siege was recorded by the Jewish historian **Josephus**. Part of the account of Josephus includes the words of the leader of the Jews besieged in Masada: 'It is clear that at daybreak our resistance will come to an end. But we are free to choose an honourable way to die with those we love. Let us die without becoming **slaves** to our enemies.'

'On top of this [the ramp that the Romans had constructed] they constructed a pier of stones. On this they built a tower 90 feet [27.5 m] high protected all over with plates of iron. This tower was for the ballistas and stone-throwers. Silva also organized a great battering ram to be swung continuously against the wall until it was beaten in one place.'
Josephus

 This saucepan is similar in design to ones used in the kitchen, but this example is made of silver and has an inscription on its handle to the mother goddess. It was probably used for pouring out offerings of wine to the gods.

Meals

For those Romans who were rich enough, meals were tasty and varied. There were usually three meals a day. At dawn the **family** would breakfast (called *ientaculum*) on bread and fruit. A light meal, the *prandium*, was taken at midday and usually consisted of cold meat, fish, vegetables and bread. The main meal of the day (the *cena*) began at about 8 pm and its various courses could go on well into the evening.

This main meal was divided into three courses. The *gustatio* was literally a taster and had a variety of dishes made from eggs, fish or vegetables. Popular dishes were oysters, snails fed on milk and stuffed dormice. Honeyed wine, called *mulsum*, might be served with this course. The main course, or the *primae mensae*, had a variety of roast or boiled meats and poultry. Often these dishes were plain, such as stew or sausages, but for special occasions and feasts there were exotic dishes such as boiled ostrich. The meal finished with a sweet course, known as the *secundae mensae*, which was often just fruit. At home, diners would recline on couches and eat from low tables (see **Food**).

If you were poor, your diet probably consisted of beans and lentils, perhaps a little meat, and certainly bread.

Sausages
Chop up the meat and pound with white bread which has had the crust removed and has been soaked in wine. Pound pepper, liquamen and, if you like, myrtle berries. Make little forcemeat balls, inserting pine kernels and peppercorns. Wrap in sausage skin and cook gently in reduced wine.
Apicius

Honeyed bread
Remove the crust from a wholewheat loaf and break into largish pieces. Soak them in milk, fry in oil, then pour honey over and serve.
Apicius

Metal working

Like many other ancient peoples, the Romans dug mines to excavate the rock in which metal ore was found. The rocks were pounded, sometimes with **battering rams**, to extract the ore. The ore was then smelted with charcoal in a furnace and the metal poured out. The Romans extracted lead this way for use in making water pipes, for example. But the two main metals for making a range of objects were iron and bronze. Roman blacksmiths never discovered how to get

This silver hairpin has been made in the shape of a hand holding a pomegranate.

a temperature hot enough to make cast iron – that is, pouring molten iron into moulds. The blacksmith heated iron pieces in a forge and hammered them into shape. Many everyday objects, tools, **weapons** and **machinery** were made from iron. Some smiths specialized in working in bronze, which was a mixture of copper and tin. Because they could heat bronze to the right temperature, bronze smiths poured their molten metal into moulds. Many objects were made this way, from hairpins to **statues**. The wealthy could have objects such as hairpins made of silver or jewellery made of gold.

Minerva

Minerva was the **goddess** of wisdom, crafts, industries and trade. As the goddess of the arts she was said to have been the inventor of musical instruments, especially wind instruments. Flute players held a feast-day in her honour on 13 June each year, but her main festival was held in March and lasted for five days. Minerva also guided soldiers in war, and she is often shown with a helmet and wearing armour. Soldiers often wore her image on their armour to protect them from harm.

*Left: This is the tombstone of a man who lived in Rome around the beginning of the 1st century AD. The inscription reads 'P. Curtilius, freedman of Publius, silversmith'. He is shown with a small chisel and mallet (in his right hand) working on a metal vessel. (For freedmen and freedwomen, see **Slaves**.)*

Above: This bar, called a pig, is made of lead and it was the way metal was transported in bulk before being made into objects such as pipes or roofing material. There were lead mines in a number of places in Britain; this bar was made in AD 76 and comes from north Wales.

93

This marble statue shows the god Mithras, who originated in the East (modern Iran) killing a bull

You would have to break this pottery money box jar if you wanted to take out your savings.

Mithras

The worship of the Persian **god** Mithras was originally brought to **Rome** in the 1st century AD. His worship was associated with the struggle between good and evil. He is often pictured killing a bull, whose flowing blood was thought to be the source of life. Worship of Mithras was for men only, especially by soldiers and merchants all over the **empire**. **Temples** to Mithras has been found in **London** and on **Hadrian's Wall**, for example.

Money

The Romans minted several different value coins. Worth the most was the gold *aureus*, which was worth 100 of the value of an *as*. The *dupondius* was worth two *asses*, the *sestertius* four *asses* and the *denarius* sixteen *asses*. The *as* was divided into four coins called *quadrans*. At the time of the **empire**, coins carried the portrait of the **emperor** with his titles. The reverse of the coin might record some great event, such as the emperor **Claudius**'s conquest of **Britain**.

These gold coins were buried in Britain by a soldier in Claudius's army in the invasion of AD 43. These thirty-seven coins represent more than four years' pay for an ordinary legionary soldier.

A mosaic from one of the living rooms in the house of a wealthy person living in Italica.

This mosaic covered the dining room of the Roman villa at Hinton St Mary in Britain. In the centre of the design is a representation of the head of Christ (see **Christianity**).

Mosaics

The most famous and impressive examples of all Roman interior decoration are mosaics.

Mosaics are patterns or pictures created in stone, or other materials, and laid on floors or walls and ceilings. Once a flat, even surface had been prepared, the pattern or design for the picture was scratched out. Small cubes of cut stone or tile, called *tesserae*, were then laid in mortar (a mix of sand, lime and water). Simple designs and the most complicated pictures could all be made by a skilful mosaic-maker. The more the mosaic picture needed to look like a painting the smaller the *tesserae* had to be, otherwise the detail would become lost.

Sometimes the central picture of a mosaic would be made up in the workshop and then carried to the **house**. The *tesserae* would be glued face down on to a piece of material, which was then placed face up in wet mortar on the floor. After the mortar had set, the material could be scraped off the picture.

At the end of the process, a mosaic floor would be ground and polished to achieve a perfectly even surface. This would help to bring out the colours of the different stones that had been used to create it.

Mosaics have been discovered all across the Roman world and they sometimes survive even when other evidence, such as the buildings themselves, have rotted away. Mosaics are often removed during archaeological excavations to help preserve them and placed on view in museums where the public can readily see them.

'It is recorded that Julius Caesar carried mosaics with him on his campaigns.'
Suetonius

Music

Music played an important part in stage plays and people could go to a concert in a little **theatre** called an *odeon*. Musicians had a choice of a number of instruments: the *lituus* was a long horn used for funeral processions and by the **army**; the *bucina* was a trumpet used mainly in the army; the *cithara* was a form of lyre and its strings were plucked; the *cornu* was a hoop-like horn used for religious processions, funerals and ceremonies. Other instruments were the *tuba* (a long trumpet), the *tibiae* (double pipes), the *fistula* (panpipes), the *cymbala* (cymbals) and the *typanum* (tambourine).

Roman musicians also used an organ (called an *hydraulis*) in which air was forced through the pipes by a water pump. This organ was used to provide music during fights between **gladiators** in the **amphitheatre**. It was also used in the theatre and some people had them installed in their own **houses**.

Myths and legends

Stories handed down from generation to generation about **gods**, people and events are often called myths or legends. The Romans told many myths, especially ones about the origins of the Roman people and the city of **Rome** itself – the legend of **Romulus and Remus**, for example. **Children** learned about the myths and legends of their people, as well as history, in what we would now call secondary school.

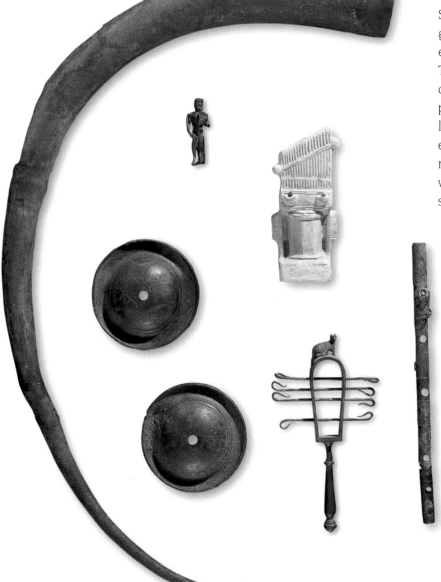

Musical instruments from the far left: trumpet, statuette of a musician holding a lyre, a pair of cymbals, a terracotta model of an organ and below it a 'sistrum', a rattle used in religious ceremonies and processions in honour of the Egyptian goddess Isis. On the right of the group of instruments is a pair of flutes.

Navy

Roman had no navy until its first war with **Carthage** in 264 BC. Even when **ships** were built they were often used as floating fighting platforms. Naval captains tried to ram the enemy's ships so that they would sink. If this tactic failed then a large ramp could be lowered on to the enemy's ship and the marines would rush across and fight hand to hand. The standard Roman warship was called a *quinquereme* and had 300 rowers on three levels and carried 120 marines. Seamen that served for twenty-six years in the navy were made Roman citizens when they were discharged.

During the reign of the emperor **Augustus** there were four fleets based at Misenum in the Bay of Naples, at Ravenna in northern Italy, in **Egypt** and in **Syria**. Later, a fleet was built for the **invasion** of **Britain**. To protect the Channel and the North Sea, two fleets (in **Latin**, *classis*) were built – the *Classis Britannica* and the *Classis Germanica*.

Nero

Nero succeeded his stepfather, the emperor **Claudius**, as head of the Roman state. Nero was a playboy with a taste for murder and cruelty. One of those he murdered was his mother, Agrippina, Claudius's wife, who had organized and fought for his succession. His reign was, at first, considered to be a good one. But he came to be dominated by others, especially his wife Poppaea. He kicked her to death only three years after they were married.

Nero was well-known for his public musical performances. It was said that he had the doors of the **theatre** locked so that the audience could not leave while he was singing or playing. In AD 64 a disastrous fire broke out and destroyed much of the centre of **Rome**. Nero was at his birthplace, Antium, on the coast when it broke out. He hurried back and organized firefighting efforts, temporary shelters and other relief measures. Despite this, people thought that he had deliberately started the fire and could not forgive him for singing one of his own compositions, *The Fall of Troy*, dressed in full stage costume, while watching the fire. The myth of Nero playing the fiddle while Rome burned probably arose from that singing.

Nero blamed the **Christians** for the fire and as a result hundreds were executed for their 'crime'. **Tacitus** wrote

'When the Romans saw that the war against the Carthaginians was dragging on, they decided for the first time to build ships, but their shipwrights were completely unused to building warships. However, one Carthaginian warship ran aground and into the hands of the Romans. They used this ship as a model to build their entire fleet.'
Polybius,
2nd century BC

The head of the emperor Nero sculpted in marble.

that many were dressed in wild **animal** skins to be killed by dogs in the **amphitheatres**. People believed that Nero started the great fire of Rome because he built a grand palace, called the Golden House, set in a huge park on the land that had been cleared by the fire. The palace had an enormous statue of Nero, 37 m (120 ft) high, in the entrance hall. It was this colossal statue that gave the largest of Rome's amphitheatres , the **Colosseum**, its name.

There were several conspiracies against Nero. Finally, in AD 68, the **legions** supported Galba, a governor in **Gaul**, in his bid to become **emperor**. Nero escaped from the soldiers but committed suicide by stabbing himself in the throat (his private secretary had to finish him off). True to his theatrical nature to the end, his final words were said to have been: 'What an artist the world is losing!'

'Good, now I can live like a human being at last.'
Nero, on the completion of his Golden House

Nîmes

The town of Nemausus (now called Nîmes) was occupied by the Romans in the late 1st century BC in one of the **provinces** of **Gaul**. It had been a Celtic (see **Druids**) and then a **Greek settlement**. It was established as a *colonia* (see **Cities and new towns**) in the reign of the emperor **Augustus**. It became one of the largest and wealthiest of the cities in southern Gaul (now the French area of Provence) with a population of about 50,000 people in the 2nd century AD.

Many Roman monuments and buildings have survived to the present day in and around Nîmes. Among these are the **aqueduct** called the Pont du Gard, the **amphitheatre** (which was large enough hold 25,000 spectators) and a **temple** known as Maison Carrée.

This bronze statuette shows the emperor Nero dressed in fine armour, which is decorated with gold and silver.

Numbers

Romans used letters to write numbers. Some of them are familiar to us today because you sometimes see them on modern inscriptions, on clocks and even in some books. Some of the letters they used come from **Latin** words – for example,

C is from *centum*, meaning 100, and M is from *mille passuum*, meaning a mile or 1000 paces. The Romans may have taken L, V, X and D from other alphabets.

To form larger numbers the Romans put letters together. This was either done by subtracting a larger number (for example IX for the number 9) or adding on (for example X1 for the number 11).

Modern number	Roman number	Latin word
1	I	uno
2	II	duo
3	III	tres
4	IIII or IV	quattuor
5	V	quinque
6	VI	sex
7	VII	septem
8	VIII	octo
9	IX or VIIII	novem
10	X	decem

Larger numbers

50=L   100=C   500=D   1000=M

To write other Roman numbers you have to put one or more together – for example:

12=XII

30=XXX

60=LX

700=DCC

2000=MM

This is the tombstone of a boy who died in the province of Britain in the early 2nd century AD. The inscription tells us that his name was Marcus Cocceius Nonnus and that he was only six (VI) years of age.

Officials

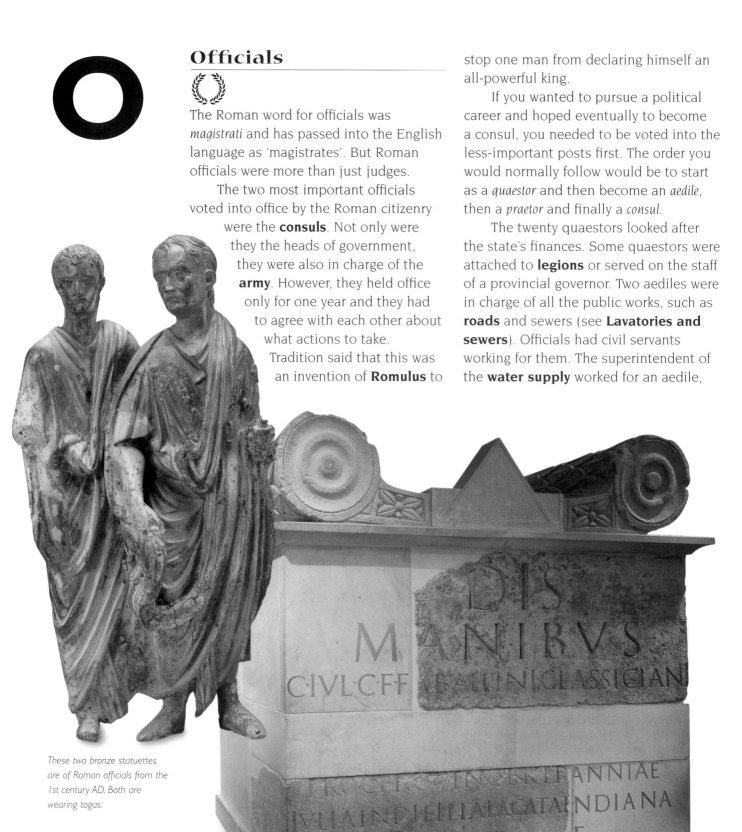

The Roman word for officials was *magistrati* and has passed into the English language as 'magistrates'. But Roman officials were more than just judges.

The two most important officials voted into office by the Roman citizenry were the **consuls**. Not only were they the heads of government, they were also in charge of the **army**. However, they held office only for one year and they had to agree with each other about what actions to take.

Tradition said that this was an invention of **Romulus** to stop one man from declaring himself an all-powerful king.

If you wanted to pursue a political career and hoped eventually to become a consul, you needed to be voted into the less-important posts first. The order you would normally follow would be to start as a *quaestor* and then become an *aedile*, then a *praetor* and finally a *consul*.

The twenty quaestors looked after the state's finances. Some quaestors were attached to **legions** or served on the staff of a provincial governor. Two aediles were in charge of all the public works, such as **roads** and sewers (see **Lavatories and sewers**). Officials had civil servants working for them. The superintendent of the **water supply** worked for an aedile,

These two bronze statuettes are of Roman officials from the 1st century AD. Both are wearing togas.

This elaborate tomb is of the official Classicianus, who was governor of the province of Britain in the 1st century AD. He was buried in London and his tomb, like many others, has the words DIS MANIBUS, 'To the spirits of the departed', carved on it.

for example. Next on the political ladder came the praetors, eventually eight in number. Praetors were the state's chief judges. Ex-consuls and ex-praetors were often given a **province** to govern.

There were also two censors, who kept the official census of citizens and who could strike someone's name off the census. Tribunes were elected to look after the interests of the ordinary people, the **plebeians**, but some served as senior officers in the army. Procurators usually served on the staff of a governor of a province to look after the finances.

Olives and olive oil

Olives were an important crop for the ancient **Greeks** and the Romans. Olive trees are still a common sight in the Mediterranean area. The trees provided a **crop** that could be eaten and pressed into oil. The oil was used mainly for cooking but it was also needed for lighting lamps and for rubbing into the skin in the **baths** or by athletes in competitions. Olive oil was also used in medicine and **cosmetics**. The Romans thought that the best oil came from green olives.

Although most farmers in Italy and the **provinces** around the Mediterranean Sea grew some olive trees, it was much more profitable to plant them in very large quantities. A number of specialist olive **farms** have been found in north **Africa**, for example. The writer Cato tells us that a farmer who wanted to invest in olive growing should plant 65 ha (160 acres) of trees and would need a **slave** overseer, his wife, five slaves to work on the farm, three ox-drivers, one ass-driver, and men to look after the pigs and sheep who would feed under the trees. An olive farm also needed a range of buildings to store, crush (using large stone mills) and press the olive crop. Large containers, such as **amphorae**, were also needed to

Olives were grown in many provinces in the Mediterranean area of the Roman empire.

store the oil and transport it to markets or **ports** for loading on to **ships**.

Olives and olive oil were exported from various provinces across the **empire**. Provinces in the north, which could not grow olive trees, particularly wanted this product. We know, for example, that olive oil was being imported from southern Spain into southern **Britain** even before the Romans invaded. The trade continued from Spain, but later oil from north Africa was imported in large quantities. Amphorae containing 76 litres (20 gallons) of oil, and the preserved stones of olives have been found on a number of excavations in important cities in Britain.

'The tax collector shall exact ... for a camel-load of dried foodstuffs ... for purple wool by the fleece ... for myrrh imported in goatskins ... for each donkey-load of olive oil.' Customs regulations, Palmyra, AD 137

Onager

The onager (in **Latin** this is the word for 'donkey') was a stone-throwing **siege** machine that could pound the walls of an enemy's town.

Ostia

Ostia lies on the mouth of the River Tiber, 25 km (15½ miles) from **Rome** and was the capital's **port**. By the 2nd century AD, about 50,000 people lived in Ostia. The main shipping firms based themselves here and built great warehouses for the goods and produce that passed through the port. Sixty-one of the wealthy shipping merchants and other trades that were connected with shipping built themselves a chamber of commerce in the centre of Ostia. It had been the base for the Roman **navy** until the reign of the emperor **Augustus**. Slightly up river, the Romans built another port, which they called Portus. The emperor **Claudius** began work to create an artificial harbour here to cope with the enormous increase in trade. A harbour of more than 69 ha (170 acres) was dredged out of the river bank and a ship from **Egypt** was sunk to provide a breakwater. In AD 103, fifty years later, the emperor **Trajan** made this harbour even bigger and connected it to Ostia by digging a deep channel.

Ottoman Turks

The Byzantine empire – the Holy Christian empire – developed from the

One of the streets in Ostia with apartment blocks and shops.

eastern Roman **empire** and had its capital city at **Constantinople**. Byzantium is the name we now use for the city of Constantinople (modern-day Istanbul).

This empire was under threat from the Islamic peoples in the east. The Byzantines held out against them, but on 23 May 1453 the Ottoman Turks, who came from the area of the Caspian Sea, captured Constantinople.

Ovid

The poet we know as Ovid (Publius Ovidius Naso) wrote during the reign of the emperor **Augustus**. The **emperor** disapproved of Ovid's poems and his behaviour and exiled him to Tomi, on the Black Sea. Ovid missed life in the capital of the **empire** and wrote *Laments* and *Letters from the Black Sea*. He is better known for his poems, the *Metamorphoses*, a collection of Greek and Roman mythological stories, and *The Art of Love*.

The church of Hagia Sophia (Holy Wisdom) was built by the emperor Justinian in Constantinople and was consecrated in AD 537. This church was the first to be converted into a mosque by the Ottoman Turks. The inset picture is The Blue Mosque in Istanbul, built between 1609 and 1616 by Sultan Ahmet I to surpass Hagia Sophia.

P

Palla

The palla is a woman's outer garment worn in Roman times to cover the body and head. This garment could be described as the female equivalent to a man's **toga**. It was draped to allow one hand to be kept free.

Palmyra

Palmyra was an oasis (a fertile place) in the Syrian Desert. It was a caravan city serving the needs of camel and donkey trains bringing luxury goods from India, China and Arabia to the coastal **ports** of the **province** of **Syria**.

The city was brought under Roman control in 18 AD. In the 2nd century AD a whole series of public **buildings** were constructed, including a magnificent street lined with columns

that ran for nearly 1 km (⅔ mile) across the city. The **forum** of the city must have been the place where the camels were unloaded.

Many stone **sculptures** of finely dressed Palmyrene men and women have been found throughout the **empire**.

Patricians

Romans were divided into three classes: **plebeians**, **equites** and patricians. The patricians traced their ancestry back to the noble families of ancient **Rome**. They were the privileged class in Roman society. Until 445 BC patricians were not allowed by law to marry plebeians.

A monumental arch built at the end of a colonnaded street in Palmyra.

This relief carving in marble has as its subject a small coastal ship, called a 'corbita'. These vessels hauled goods and produce along the coasts of the Mediterranean countries of the Roman empire. Pausanias also travelled in ships like this to study the coastlines of Greece.

Pausanias

We know very little about the life of the Greek doctor Pausanias, who became a traveller and geographer at the time of the emperor **Hadrian**. He did leave a ten-book tourist guide to the antiquities and ancient sites of **Greece**. This work, *Description of Greece*, contains invaluable information about sites, **statues** and customs that are now lost.

Pets

The Romans kept pets, mainly for their **children**, as well as guard dogs with names like *Ferox* (Fierce) and *Celer* (Swift). Cats and birds were also kept as pets.

Plautus

We know of twenty-one comic plays that were written by Plautus. Plautus came from Umbria in central Italy and originally worked in the **theatre** in **Rome**. With the money he earned he set himself up in business but then lost everything and had to work in a flour mill. While he worked as a labourer he wrote three plays. Audiences loved his comedies and even after his death in 184 BC his plays continued to be performed and enjoyed.

Perhaps audiences throughout the **empire** loved Plautus's plays because they had stories and characters ordinary Romans could recognize. His play *The Rope*, for example, tells the story of a young man who falls in love with a slave girl and, of course, they are not allowed to marry. But the play has a happy ending. The girl turns out to be free-born – a secret revealed when documents in a trunk, with a rope attached, are washed up on the shore.

This mosaic of a dog, perhaps a hunting dog, comes from the entrance hall of a house in Halicarnassus (now in modern Turkey) and was created in the 4th century AD.

This mosaic from Pompeii shows actors preparing for a performance. The playwright is probably the one who is sitting and he is surrounded by actors dressing in their costumes, putting masks on and rehearsing dance and music.

Playwrights

Theatre audiences in the Roman world were very familiar with **Greek** playwrights, both those who wrote serious plays (tragedies) and comedies. We do not know the names of most of the Roman playwrights whose plays were performed in theatres in **Rome** and throughout the **provinces**. The scripts of very few entire plays have survived. Two famous and popular Roman playwrights are **Plautus** and Terentius (known today as Terence).

Terence lived in the 2nd century BC and came from north **Africa** to Rome as a slave. He got his Roman name from his master, a Roman senator called Terentius Lucanus, who educated him and encouraged him to write.

Plebeians

Romans were divided into three social classes: plebeians, **equites** and **patricians**. The plebeians (in **Latin** the word is *plebs*) were the ordinary working people. They could vote but could not hold high office, such as that of the **consuls** (see also **Officials**).

The historian Dionysius, who came from the city of Halicarnassus in the

province of **Asia** (now Turkey), tells how **Romulus** decided how Roman society should be organized. He wrote: 'The patricians were to serve as priests, officials, lawyers and judges. The plebeians were to be farmers and till the land, herd animals and work for wages as craft and tradespeople and labourers.'

Pliny

There are two famous Roman writers called Pliny. Pliny the Elder held public offices and served in the **army**. He is well known today for his 102-volume work *Natural History*, but also because he died during the eruption of Vesuvius while trying to rescue friends in Pompeii. He was the commander of the Roman fleet stationed at the nearby **port** of Misenum.

His nephew, whom we know as Pliny the Younger, also held public offices and was a writer. His letters, which were published, are an important source of information about Roman life, customs and events. He gives us the written record for the destruction of **Pompeii and Herculaneum** in AD 79, for example.

Some letters from Pliny the Younger are to the emperor **Trajan** asking for advice when he was sent as the governor of a **province** of Bithynia and Pontus on the coast of the Black Sea (see map on page 5). For example, Pliny is concerned about recent devastating fires in the city of Nicomedia that destroyed 'many private **houses** and two public **buildings**'. Pliny asks Trajan for permission to establish an organized service of 150 firefighters. Trajan's reply shows a concern that organizations such as this 'soon become political groups' and suggests that Pliny 'buy equipment which can be used to put out fires and to tell the property owners to use it themselves and, if necessary, the crowd that gathers to watch the fire'.

Pompeii and Herculaneum

One of the worst disasters in Roman history happened when the volcano Mount Vesuvius erupted in AD 79. Two important towns on the Bay of Naples, Pompeii and Herculaneum, were both destroyed by the eruption. Most of the population escaped but everyone in these cities and nearby lost their homes. The eruption of the volcano was so strong that a thin layer of ash fell on the city of Naples 15 km (9 miles) away. Pompeii was covered with ash and stones nearly 4 m (13 ft) deep; Herculaneum was filled with a huge mudflow. At the same time, the writer **Pliny** the Younger was staying with his uncle, the commander of the Roman fleet stationed at the nearby **port**

The archaeologist Guiseppe Fiorelli, who was appointed as the new director of excavations at Pompeii in 1860, came up with the idea of pouring plaster into holes he discovered. This is one of the many casts he made of people, animals and objects that had rotted away leaving cavities in the hardened ash.

Above: Today you can walk freely down the main streets in Pompeii, looking into the remains of the shops and houses on either side. Notice the stepping stones here, which allowed people to cross the street without getting their feet wet and muddy during rainy weather.

Left: The ruins of houses in Herculaneum, which, along with Pompeii, was destroyed when Mount Vesuvius erupted in AD 79.

The volcano Mount Vesuvius
towers over the modern town
of Resina in Italy, with ancient
Herculaneum in the foreground.

of Misenum, and witnessed the eruption. Pliny wrote: 'On 24 August at about 1 pm, my mother pointed out to uncle an odd-shaped cloud. We couldn't make out which mountain it came from but later found out it was from Vesuvius. The cloud was rising in a shape rather like a pine tree because it shot up to a great height in the form of a tree trunk, then spread out at the top into branches.'

When his uncle received reports that people were in danger, he sent in the fleet to rescue them. Pliny tells us that his uncle died, suffocated by the sulphur fumes, trying to get back to his ship. It took about three days for the sky to clear, but by then it was impossible for anybody to live in the towns. The emperor Titus gave money to help the homeless, but the towns were never rebuilt.

The tragedy did at least provide us with some remarkable evidence for Roman life in the 1st century AD. The towns were rediscovered in 1594, and by the 18th century excavations had begun. Now modern visitors can walk around the

Below: This elaborate summer dining room is in a house in Herculaneum called the House of Neptune and has mosaics on the walls. Neptune, the god of water, and the sea goddess Amphitrite can be seen in more detail in the inset photograph on the right .

A plaster cast of a wooden window shutter in a house in the ruined city of Pompeii.

The remains of a bakery in Pompeii showing the oven on the left (where carbonized bread was found intact) and the huge millstones for grinding grain into flour on the right.

ruins and some buildings, especially in Herculaneum, are very well preserved. Thousands of objects have been recovered and excavators even found bread, which had been burned and turned into carbon, perfectly preserved in an oven in a baker's shop in Pompeii. The bread had been freshly baked ready for customers in the afternoon of 24 August AD 79. The excavation of this bakery in the late 19th century caused great excitement, and drawings of people taking the preserved bread from the oven appeared in newspapers and magazines.

Pompey

Gnaius Pompeius (Pompey) was a Roman general and politician, born in 106 BC. He fought with **Sulla** against **Marius** in the **civil war** and added *Magnus* ('the Great') to his name after victory in **Africa**. He campaigned in the eastern Mediterranean against King Mithradates VI and won back the **province** of **Asia** for **Rome** in 63 BC. He also cleared the seas of large bands of pirates in 67 BC. He was one of the three men (called the Triumvirate) to govern

Rome – the others were Crassus and **Julius Caesar** – and married Caesar's daughter. He was jealous of Caesar and caused the civil war, taking the side of the **senate**. After his defeat at the battle of Pharsalus by Caesar he fled to **Egypt**, but was murdered there in 48 BC.

This coin of Pompey the Great was minted by his son, Sextus Pompey, in 38 BC.

Ports

Trade was essential to the wealth of the Roman **empire**. Safe and deep anchorage was needed for merchant **ships** and the **navy** along the coasts of the empire. All over the Roman world engineers and builders constructed harbours, and **ports** grew up around them. The architect **Vitruvius** laid down recommended materials and methods for building these harbours. Remains of Roman harbours survive all over the Mediterranean, and others have been excavated in **provinces** further away – for example in **London** and at **Leptis Magna**. The most important was **Ostia**, the port of **Rome**.

Pottery

The most common objects archaeologists are likely to find on an excavation are pieces of broken **pottery**. Clay was the basic material for large numbers of kitchen utensils – storage jars, such as transport vessels (**amphorae**), cooking pots and even funnels and colanders – as well as plates and bowls for serving and eating. Some bowls were very highly decorated – perhaps made in a carved mould or painted with designs or scenes.

Clay was specially prepared, moulded or thrown on a potter's wheel, shaped and then fired in large batches in kilns. The same method was used to make **tiles** for building. Some types of pottery, such as the shiny red pottery from **Gaul**, Italy and north **Africa**, were made in very large quantities for people living in the cities.

This pot was made to hold the cremated remains of a body. The name Colchester and a museum number were put on it after excavation.

A group of jars, dishes and bowls for the dining table found in Britain. Some were imported from Gaul (the red dish) but the others were made in Britain.

Priests and priestesses

Worship of **gods and goddesses** usually involved processions to a **temple** and making **sacrifices** and offerings at an altar. The *pontifex* (the **Latin** word for priest) carried out the ceremony for the worshippers. An official, called the *pontifex maximus* (chief priest) conducted the ceremony on behalf of the Roman state.

There was a very large number of religious festivals held throughout the Roman year involving special ceremonies and sporting competitions. For example, in January alone there were thirty-two individual religious festivals, including horse races in honour of the god **Mars**; the festival of **Vesta**, goddess of the sacred fire; the sacrifice of bulls to the goddess Earth; a purification of the shields sacred to Mars, the god of war; and festivals to the gods of pasture land, mildew and boundaries.

An altar found at Chester, Britain. It was in a temple and was dedicated to Aesculapius, the god of healing, to Salus, the goddess of health and to Fortuna, the goddess of good luck.

113

Part of a mosaic from the floor of a dining room in a house in Cathage in north Africa. It is wonderfully detailed and shows baskets overflowing with fish and flowers. It was made in the 2nd century AD.

Provinces

When the Romans were at war with the **Carthaginians** the area they controlled was not much greater than Italy itself. Areas that came under the control of Rome were called provinces – the islands of Sicily and Sardinia, for example. The provinces were governed by specially elected **officials**.

By the time of **Julius Caesar** the Roman state had increased enormously in size, so much so that most of the Mediterranean Sea was ringed by lands – provinces – governed by **Rome**. Provinces were added by **invasion** and treaty – from Sicily in 241 BC to **Arabia** and Dacia in AD 106, for example.

Some large provinces were divided into smaller territories so they could be more easily governed and controlled. The province of **Germany** was divided into Lower Germany and Upper Germany, for example.

Produce

An enormous amount of **food** was needed to feed the 60 million inhabitants of the Roman **empire**. Much of this food was grown, sold and eaten locally, but a great deal had to be imported (see **Import/export**) from the **provinces** into the big cities of Italy and throughout the rest of the empire.

In addition to the food for sale in markets and **shops**, huge amounts of grain were needed to make into bread to feed the poor of **Rome**. Approximately 200,000 people were registered for free food handouts by 2 BC.

The grain came from the rich farmlands of provinces such as **Egypt** and from Sicily. There was also demand in Rome for animals, vegetables, fruit and herbs.

The subject of this mosaic is sacks of grapes being brought in from the vineyard. The mosaic was discovered in a house at Augusta, now Paphos, which was the Roman capital of the Greek island of Cyprus.

Republic

The word 'republic' is used today to mean a system of government in which the head of state (for example, the president) is elected by the citizens. The Roman name was *res publica*, meaning 'a matter for the people'. Each year, Roman citizens voted for two heads of state, called **consuls** (see **Officials**). The **senate** was like a modern parliament.

The Roman republic was established in 509 BC, when the last king, **Tarquin the Proud**, was thrown out of the city because of his cruelty and arrogance.

Roads

The Romans needed a large and complex network of roads to link their **cities**, to transport produce from the countryside to the towns, to export manufactured goods across the **empire** and, not least, to allow easy and rapid access to all parts of the Roman world for their **armies**. People on official business used the **cursus publicus** to get about the empire.

The empire's road system began at the Great **Forum** in **Rome** and was marked by a golden milestone. In the **provinces** the first roads were built by the army to help conquer new lands. Then gangs of **slaves** or local workers were used to level the ground and pound down gravel and stone to make a hard-wearing surface. Roman roads were not always straight, but the surveyors did try to go from place to place by the most direct route. Many Roman roads and city streets are still in use today, although they lie below the present surfaces.

'The emperor Trajan had this road built by cutting through mountains and eliminating the bends.'
From a milestone near the River Danube AD 100

Right: This milestone was found beside a Roman road in Wales. This one records that at this point travellers are VIII (8) Roman miles from the fort of Kanovium (now Caerhun).

Paved roads leading out of towns and cities often have tombs lining them. This is because it was unlawful to bury anyone inside the limits of Roman towns.

115

In this picture of the forum in Rome the columns on the left are from the temple built by the emperor Antoninus for his wife Faustina after she died. The three columns on the right are the remains of the temple to the twin gods Castor and Pollux.

Rome

The Romans believed that **Romulus** founded the city of Rome in 753 BC. We do know that as early as 1000 BC villages were built on some of the seven hills that later made up the area of the capital city of the Roman state. The **Etruscans** ruled the first villages of Rome. The town grew on the west bank of the River Tiber, which is the river that runs to the sea where the **port** of **Ostia** was established. The **forum** was built in around 600 BC, and the city had its first wall around 378 BC.

By the 3rd century BC there were about 100,000 inhabitants in Rome, but by the time of **Julius Caesar** this number had grown to about 1 million. Spectators, numbering as many as 100,000, could watch the chariot racing in the city's main stadium, the **Circus Maximus**. There were many public **buildings**. **Aqueducts** brought water into the city, and a network of **roads** stretched out from the centre into the Italian countryside.

The emperor **Augustus** was the first person to carry out any large-scale redevelopment of the city. He commissioned many new public buildings and **temples**. Fires were frequent in the city, especially in the poorer districts where most people lived in **apartments** that were badly built and maintained. A disastrous fire, during the reign of the emperor **Nero**, swept through ten of the fourteen districts of Rome. The forum, in

Romulus and Remus

The Romans believed the legend (see **Myths and Legends**) that Romulus, the first ruler they called *rex*, the **Latin** word meaning 'king', founded the city of **Rome** on 21 April in the year 753 BC.

Roman **children** were all told the story of Romulus and his twin brother Remus. As babies they had been cast adrift in a basket on the River Tiber by the wicked brother of their stepfather. They were saved from drowning and suckled by a she-wolf before being discovered by the kindly shepherd of the royal flocks, Faustulus. The twins were then brought up in secret by the shepherd and his wife. The boys grew up and went on to found Rome – however, in an argument over who was to rule the city, Romulus killed Remus.

Minted in around 275–260 BC, this coin pictures the story of Romulus and Remus being suckled by the she-wolf.

This bronze statue of a wolf was made by an Etruscan artist in the 6th century BC. The twins were added early in the 16th century AD, but it is likely that other figures were there originally.

imperial times, became too small to cope with all the religious ceremonies and administration of the **empire**, so new forums had to be built elsewhere in the city. By the 3rd century AD, Rome had reached its maximum size and huge walls had to be built to include the outer districts and to defend the city.

In AD 330 emperor **Constantine the Great** moved the capital of the empire to **Constantinople**, now Istanbul in Turkey. The **Goths** sacked Rome in AD 410 and by the end of that century the Roman empire in the west did not exist.

S

Sacrifices

Worshippers made offerings to **gods and goddesses** either in public **temples** or at **household shrines**. Offerings included cheese, cakes made with honey, fruit or wine or milk poured out on to the ground. **Animals** were also sacrificed to the gods. For example, a bull, a ram and a pig were sacrificed in a ceremony in **Rome** that marked the beginning of the five-yearly census, or count, of citizens. This is part of a prayer uttered when the emperor **Augustus** sacrificed a cow to the goddess **Juno**: 'O Queen Juno, let sacrifice be made to you with a splendid cow and may you grant everlasting safety, victory and health to the Roman people.'

Samnites

To establish a state for themselves, the Romans had to fight and conquer all the surrounding peoples – the Sabines in the northeast, the Aequi who lived in the mountainous area of central Italy, the **Etruscans** north of **Rome** and the Volsci who lived close to the city.

A difficult enemy for the Romans, however, were the Samnites. They were a powerful and warlike people who lived in villages in central Italy, south of Rome. Originally the Romans had signed a treaty with them to help conquer the Volsci. But a war broke out between the two peoples in 343 BC that lasted for fifty years, after which the Samnites agreed to become allies of Rome.

Saturn

The name of this **god** in **Latin** was *Saturnus* and is said to have come from the word for 'sowing'. Saturn came to be associated with sowing seeds, especially corn. The **temple** of Saturn in the Roman **forum** was also the city's central treasury.

The festival of this god, called the Saturnalia, was the merriest of the Roman year. **Slaves** were allowed temporary liberty to do as they liked, and presents were exchanged. By the 4th century AD this festival was held on New Year's Day and became part of the traditional Christmas celebrations.

School

In early **Rome**, **families** taught their sons, and sometimes their daughters, at home. A boy going into public life had to learn a range of outdoor skills and sports, as well as school subjects. He learned to fight in

One of the ways in which the Romans wrote was with a pen and ink. The owner of this inkpot, found in Roman London, scratched his name IVCVNDVS (Iucundus) on the outside.

armour, throw a javelin, ride on horseback, swim and box. Some wealthy fathers employed educated **slaves** to tutor their **children**.

Usually by the age of seven, children (mostly boys) were sent out to school. The schoolmaster, called a *magister ludi*, took a small number of fee-paying pupils. The school might be in his home or in a room he had rented. Lessons in reading, writing and arithmetic began at dawn and finished in the early afternoon.

After five years at this first school, children were taught by a better educated

'As soon as his son was old enough, Cato took him in hand and taught him to read even though he had a good slave, called Chilo, who was a schoolteacher and taught many other boys. So Cato taught his son reading and writing, the law and gymnastics, and all sorts of outdoor skills such as throwing the javelin, fighting in armour, horseriding, boxing, swimming and how to stand up to heat and cold.'
Plutarch

Made around the time of the emperor Augustus, this is a miniature bronze sculpture of a young woman. Her eyes were made from glass paste. Her ears were pierced so that earrings could be attached.

teacher called a *grammaticus*. He taught the children history, astronomy, geometry and the literature of Rome and **Greece**. They were also taught to speak clearly and had to recite texts, such as *Aesop's Fables*, in front of the class. Some schools also offered children lessons in gymnastics.

Teachers were very strict with their pupils at any age. They used a leather strap or cane if they did not attend their lessons or if they misbehaved during class.

Some young people, almost always boys, went on to the final stage of their education at sixteen years. Roman universities were centres of learning where students studied with several scholars specializing in different subjects. University teachers often gave their lectures or engaged in discussion in the open air. Many sons from wealthy families attended universities in Greece, particularly in **Athens**. This is because the Romans admired the language, literature and the culture of the **Greeks**.

Sculpture

Sculptured images of people and animals exist from across the Roman world. Roman sculpture was created mostly from carved stone, but more expensive examples could be made of melted bronze that was cast in moulds.

Statues and busts of **emperors**, **gods and goddesses** and famous people were erected in the streets, public **buildings** and **temples**. Wealthy Romans often had statues or busts of their ancestors in their homes.

Large numbers of sculptured portraits of ordinary men, **women** and **children** appear on tombstones that have survived from Roman times (see **Burials and tombstones**).

This mosaic is a sign for the offices of the NAVICULARII (shipbuilders) outside their offices in Ostia, the port of Rome. The ship on the right with its special ram is a navy vessel.

Senate

The Roman senate was made up of ex-**officials**, such as the **consuls**, once they had served their period of office. Although the senators' function was to advise the officials, like the consuls, the senate was like a parliament today, in which matters of state were discussed and laws passed. Tradition said that **Romulus** created a hundred senators but by **Julius Caesar**'s time the number had reached 900. The emperor **Augustus** reduced the number drastically.

Meetings of the senate took place in the *curia*, the senate-house, and were held behind closed doors. Senators wore a special **toga** with a broad purple stripe stitched to the border, and red shoes.

Settlements

Once people began to farm land (see **Farms**) rather than hunt or collect their food, they also began to build settlements.

The Romans wished to increase their territory and, once they had conquered these foreign lands, they established villages or towns in their new countries. There were new settlements, as well as occupied existing centres, in all their new **provinces**. Some replaced Roman **forts** that were built to establish Roman rule by force – **Colchester** in **Britain** is an example of this – while others were constructed by local people who were encouraged to set up Roman-style towns in the provinces.

Ships

The Romans built boats and ships for three types of journeys: inland on **canals** and rivers; around the coasts; and ocean-going. Small boats fitted with sails worked most inland waterways as well as huge barges measuring up to 40 m (130 ft) in length on the largest rivers – the Nile, the Rhine and the Danube. Some of the merchant ships were very large and could carry enormous amounts of produce. **Amphorae** – **pottery** containers filled with oil, **wine** or fish sauce – were a very common form of storage. Merchant ships often carried as many as 6,000 amphorae and some very large ships are recorded as bringing 1,000 tonnes of grain, with cargoes of **glass**, metal and pottery from the **provinces** of **Egypt** and north **Africa** to **Ostia**.

The Romans also needed ships for their **navy** and for transporting troops. Warships were built for speed, each driven by a sail and about 300 oarsmen. A metal ram at the prow of the ship could ram a hole an enemy ship below the waterline. Warships for the Roman navy also carried 120

marines who could rush an enemy ship across ramps.

We know that naval ships could travel fast. When **Cicero** left **Athens** in a light naval unit to go to **Ephesus** (in modern Turkey) to become governor of the **province**, he set sail on 6 July in 51 BC and arrived two weeks later, even stopping at four islands on the way – a distance of well over 320 km (200 miles).

A mosaic advertisement for a firm of importers outside their offices in Ostia. A docker is loading amphorae on to a small ship.

Below: This wall painting from a villa near Pompeii shows a coastal scene. There is a pavilion overlooking the sea, a small merchant ship and a man fishing from a bridge.

This leather shoe belonged to a child who lived in Roman London. It has open latticework at the top, like a sandal, but thick soles with metal studs to make it last.

Shoes

Shoes, boots and sandals were generally made from tanned leather in Roman times. Although most people probably wore simple styles, others were very elaborate. Sandals, for example, might be openwork designs, like the 'Greek' sandals you can buy today. Ankle boots, and even high boots, were worn by working people. There are also examples of wooden clogs – either wooden-soled shoes or sandals with wooden blocks to keep the wearer out of the mud. Roman soldiers wore a special type of shoe or sandal called a *caliga*. These were specially strengthened with iron studs on the soles for marching, working and fighting. One of the best surviving collections of shoes is at Vindolanda, near **Hadrian's Wall**.

Shops

There were no Roman supermarkets as we have today. Instead, there were lots of small shops and street stalls for most of the things a **family** might want to buy, as well as large market buildings for a number of different shopkeepers. The emperor **Trajan** built a large market building in **Rome**. The **playwright Plautus** lists a variety of shopkeepers in one of his plays – clothes-cleaner, wool-seller, jeweller, haberdasher, dyer, shoemaker, weaver, lace-seller and cabinet maker. There were also plenty

Below: A shop at a crossroads in Herculaneum (see page 108) with a public water supply and fountain nearby.

Right: A shop selling fish in the port city of Ostia.

'Zosimus sells pots, particularly for liquamen'

'The best strained liquamen *from the* factory of Umbricius Agathopus'

Advertisements found at Pompeii

This is one of the modern reconstructions of ancient sites and buildings at the Archeodrome in France. This is part of the siege works built by Julius Caesar's troops in his campaigns in Gaul to overcome the chieftain Vercingetorix in the defended town of Alesia in 52 BC.

of butchers, grocers and greengrocers and any number of bakers (see **Food**).

Perhaps the biggest difference between Roman and modern shops is that most shopkeepers made the **produce** or wares they were selling. A baker, for example, would grind his own flour using a huge millstone turned by a donkey, make the dough, bake the bread and then sell it. Inspectors made sure that shopkeepers sold the right weights and measures and charged the right price. Shops did not have windows but opened directly on to the street. The shopkeepers announced what they had to sell with painted advertisements on the outside walls of their shops.

Sieges

A siege is a military tactic to encircle a town or enemy **fort** and starve or beat those inside into surrender. The Romans were skilled at siege warfare and many famous sieges were recorded by historians – for example, **Julius Caesar's** siege of Marseilles in 49 BC during the **civil war** and the emperor **Vespasian's** governor Flavius Silva's siege of the Jewish stronghold of **Masada** in AD 73, recorded by the historian **Josephus**. The siege of Sarmizegetusa, the native capital of the Roman **province** of Dacia, is pictured on **Trajan's Column** in **Rome**.

The Romans built specialized equipment for sieges. They had a great rock-hurling machine, called an **onager** (meaning 'wild ass'), and they used **battering rams**, flame throwers and crossbows (**ballista** or catapulta) firing rocks or iron-tipped bolts. They could also undermine walls and climb over them using tall scaling towers. Roman soldiers could also adopt a special formation called a *testudo* (see page 16) to get close to walls or gates. The soldiers put their shields over their heads and around their sides so that they were completely protected from enemy missiles.

A member of a re-enactment group playing the role of the signifer and displaying the standards of the legion.

A member of a re-enactment group is seen here carrying the vexillum, the emblem of the legion. It has the legion's number, LEG XX, and its symbol, a charging boar. The signifer stands on his right in front of a troop of legionary soldiers.

Signifer

The soldier who carried the standards of each unit of about eighty men (called a *centuria*) of a **legion** in the Roman **army** was called the *signifer*. He rallied the troops, who could see the emblems of the unit on his long spear held up above the battle. This officer also acted as the banker for his unit of men.

Slaves

Slavery was very common in the ancient world. In the Roman **empire** large numbers of slaves were needed to keep society going and slaves worked in houses, in workshops and mines. An educated slave might be prized as a private tutor or a secretary.

People were enslaved in various ways: by being captured in war, by selling themselves because of debt, or by being convicted of crimes. **Children** might be sold off by their families who were too poor to keep them, and people were encouraged to collect abandoned children and bring them up as slaves. Children born to slave mothers became the slave property of the masters. Slaves were bought and sold in auctions. The Roman state owned slaves who worked on maintaining public **buildings**, such as repairing **aqueducts**.

Some slaves were treated very badly and could, by law, be punished by their

This metal tag has an inscription on it that reads, 'Hold me if I run away and return me to my master Viventius on the estate of Callistus'. It is thought to be a tag attached to a slave or a dog.

masters harshly for the smallest of mistakes. They could, for example, be put to death for running away, burned alive, crucified or sold on to the **gladiatorial** shows and hunted by wild **animals** in the arena. Once caught, even the more fortunate runaways might be branded, often on their faces, or have metal collars attached around their necks.

However, many masters and mistresses treated their slaves well, and laws were passed to put a stop to brutal treatment. But slaves still had to put up with the moods of their owners. Slaves were sometimes given their freedom in their master's will. Once freed, they did not have the same rights as citizens but their children did become full citizens.

There were large numbers of freed slaves in the Roman world, and many went on to run their own businesses in towns or **farms** in the country. Slaves could also be adopted into a **family**.

Split

Split (formerly Spalato), overlooking the Adriatic Sea in the Roman **province** of Dalmatia (modern Croatia), was the place chosen by the emperor **Diocletian** for his huge palace, which he built between AD 300 and 306. It was near where he had been born, and he intended to retire there. The palace was laid out like a Roman **fort**, with the two main streets crossing each other, and covered 39,000 sq m (400,000 sq ft). Almost half the area was taken up with **barracks** for soldiers and the whole palace was protected by a high stone wall and a number of guard towers. Inside there were palace buildings but also a **temple** to **Jupiter**, a mausoleum (an elaborate building for burial) for Diocletian, a **basilica** and **baths**.

'Here lies Vitalis, slave of Gaius Lavius Faustus and also his son, a slave born in his home.'
From a gravestone found near Philippi in Macedonia

'If the mistress of the house is in a filthy mood because there is a curl out of place, then the slave girl who is doing her hair will have her own hair torn, her tunic ripped and she will be beaten with a strap.'
Juvenal

Diocletian's palace at Spalato (now called Split) seen from the Adriatic Sea. Behind the trees you can see one of the four walls that protected his magnificent palace.

Stagecoaches

There were various forms of transport for travellers using the main **roads** through the Roman **empire**. Some went by horseback. If you were rich enough you used a *lectica* – an enclosed litter carried by four strong bearers. Ordinary travellers usually went by stagecoach. This was a four-wheeled covered wagon with other seats on top. Journeys were slow, bumpy and dirty. By comparison, the riders for the imperial mail of the **cursus publicus** could cover 70 km (43 miles) each day.

Statues

All over Roman **cities and towns**, and in homes as well, were large numbers of statues put up to honour gods, **emperors** and famous citizens. There were statues of **gods and goddesses** in their **temples** and these statues were painted and clothed, not colourless as we tend to see them today in museums. A **family** would keep busts (head and shoulders) of ancestors at shrines in their **houses** and make **sacrifices** to them.

Strabo

Strabo was a **Greek** scholar from the Roman **province** of Pontus in the east of the **empire**. He was a historian and geographer, born in about 64 BC. His *General History* has not survived but the seventeen books of his *Geography* are a mine of information about many aspects of the ancient world.

Suetonius

Suetonius came from a wealthy Roman family and worked as a lawyer. He was at one time secretary to the emperor **Hadrian**. His most important work was the book *Lives of the Twelve Caesars*, which comprises biographies of **Julius Caesar** and the first eleven **emperors** from **Augustus** to Domitian.

Sulla

Lucius Cornelius Sulla brought about **civil war** in 83 BC when he marched on Rome at the head of an **army** to overthrow the government, which had declared him a 'public enemy'. Later he secured the title of **dictator** and held this office from 82–79 BC.

This head from the province of Asia is thought to be of Sulla. It was made in bronze in the 1st century BC. Statues were made from a variety of materials – stone, bronze, ivory and even wood. Parts were sometimes gilded and painted and they were often clothed, perhaps for special occasions or religious ceremonies.

Inset left: Roman surveyors working for the army often had to do their job in difficult conditions. The walls of this fort were built high up in the rainy hills of northern Britain. Even so, the surveyors set out straight lines and perfect angles at Hardknott fort.

More surveyors were employed building roads in the provinces than on any other type of engineering projects. Although not all Roman roads are straight – the natural terrain would not always allow it – the surveyors did try to construct as direct a route as possible. This is a section of the main Roman road, called Watling Street, that runs through the Midlands of Britain.

Surveyors, architects and builders needed specialist tools to do their jobs. Here you can see a square (right), used to draw out a perfect right-angle, and a pair of dividers (left), used for making small measurements on a plan or on stone.

Surveyors

Anyone responsible for public **buildings** or **road** construction in the Roman world needed the skills of surveyors. Therefore, the ability to make accurate and careful measurements was essential.

Surveyors had a number of instruments to help them in their work. The most important of these was called a *groma*. This had two arms set at right angles with hanging plumb bobs set on a post. It allowed the surveyor to sight a straight line and then, if needed, to sight one at a right angle. Another instrument, the *groma*, could be used to mark out a road across long distances or set out the walls of a building.

A more complex instrument used to sight level lines was called the *dioptra*. It was like a surveyor's level or theodolite of today. The Romans also used an instrument much like a spirit level. It was called a *chorobates* and was used to check that floors and walls were level.

Syria

The **province** of Syria had been brought under Roman control by **Pompey** in 64 BC. The emperor **Trajan** established a frontier for the **empire** on the eastern edge of **Arabia** and Syria. A network of **roads** was laid out with **forts** built at regular intervals. Six **legions** were based here to pacify the local people and protect the frontier.

The main city of the province was called Antioch, which was built on a main trade route to the province of **Asia**. **Palmyra** was also an important city in the province and many of the **buildings** the Romans built survive today as ruins.

T

Tacitus

Tacitus was a lawyer and politician who came from a distinguished Roman **family**. He is well known today as one of **Rome's** most important historians. He wrote two great works of history in thirty books covering the years AD 14 to 96. He also wrote a biography of his father-in-law, Agricola, who was one of the governors of the **province** of **Britain**, and a book about the customs and life of the tribes in **Germany**, which had been conquered by the Romans.

Tarquin the Proud

Before the Roman **republic** was formed, parts of Italy were occupied by different peoples with their own rulers. **Rome** itself had kings who were from the Latin, the Sabine and the **Etruscan** peoples.

The last Etruscan king of Rome was called Lucius Tarquinius. The people of Rome hated him and his arrogant style of rule and they nicknamed him Tarquin the Proud. Opposition grew until a group of Roman aristocrats rose up against Tarquin in 509 BC and established the government known as the republic.

Temples

In the centre of **cities and new towns** fine temples would be built for all the important **gods and goddesses**, as well as those considered special to the people of that town. The emperor **Hadrian** completed a very famous domed temple in **Rome** called the Pantheon, which was dedicated to all the gods.

Temples usually had grand entrances with columns, and the whole building would normally be built on a raised platform to

'To the god Silvanus, the King of the Woods. Cintusmus the coppersmith willingly and gladly carries out his obligation.'
From a plaque in a temple in Colchester in Britain recording an act (not specified) by the god Silvanus for which a coppersmith has probably made a sacrifice or an offering

A Roman temple built in the time of the emperor Augustus in Nemausus (now Nîmes), in Gaul (modern France). It was dedicated to the worship of the emperor and stood at one end of the town's forum. The plan of the temple below shows its two main parts – the porch and the cella where the statue of the god or goddess would be kept.

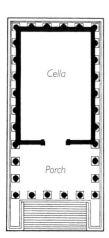

Cella

Porch

This massive temple was dedicated to the god Bacchus and was built at Heliopolis (Baalbek) in the Roman province of Syria, now in Lebanon.

make it stand out from other buildings. At the far end would be a statue of the god or goddess to whom the temple was dedicated. In some temples, worshippers would put up little plaques of thanks to the god for help they had received. Sacrifices were usually made outdoors at open-air altars.

This temple in Rome is called the Pantheon, 'to all the gods', and was built in this form by the emperor Hadrian between AD 118 and 125. The building has survived almost perfectly because it has been used as a Christian church since AD 609.

A Roman odeon built on the side of the Acropolis in Athens. It was used for recitals and concerts and was paid for by a wealthy Athenian who went on to become a consul. He built many public buildings in Athens and other Greek cities. His theatre in Athens is so well preserved that performances of plays are still put on here every year.

'On either side of the stage are the spaces for scenery. These are called periakoi **in Greek from the three-sided machines which revolve, giving a different scene on each side. These turn and present a different view to the audience when there are changes in the play or when the gods appear with sudden claps of thunder.'**
The architect Vitruvius

'It was forbidden to leave the theatre during a recital by the emperor Nero – however urgent the reason – and the gates were kept locked. We read of women in the audience giving birth and of men who were so bored with the music that they pretended to be dead and were carried away to be buried!'
Suetonius

Theatres

The Romans enjoyed Greek and Roman plays and their theatre buildings were similar to those of ancient **Greece**. At first, Roman theatres put on just serious Greek plays, called tragedies, and Greek comedies. Then Roman plays were written. There were four types of play you could see in a Roman theatre. *Fabula Palliata* was copied from Greek plays and the actors wore Greek dress. The word *fabula* in **Latin** means 'story' or 'play'. *Fabula Atellana* was a slapstick farce set in the countryside. This type of play featured well-known, and much-loved, characters, such as the clown *Bucco*, and the silly old man *Pappus*. *Fabula Praetexta* was a serious play based on a historical event or legend. Finally, *Fabula Togata* was a comedy based on village life.

Roman audiences also enjoyed a type of sketch called a *mimus*, in which women were allowed to act. These sketches contained a lot of mimicry or imitation of animals, birds and people (often very rude), and also contained

singing and dancing. The *pantomimus* was not like the pantomime we are familiar with, but was a ballet with music. There was only one actor who changed and mimed all the characters in a well-known tale or legend from the past.

Roman theatres were D-shaped **buildings**, often built into a steep hillside so the audience could more easily see the stage below. Spectators brought cushions to cover the hard, stone seats. The stage building was elaborate and looked like the outside of some grand public building. 'Sets' were also built, just as we see today in theatres, to represent particular scenes. Roman plays also demanded various devices and **machinery** – trap doors and hoists for lifting actors off the stage, for example.

Theatre audiences in Roman times could be extremely large. The theatre at **Pompeii**, for example, could hold more than 5,000 people. Theatres often had an awning to protect the audience from the sun and rain. There was also a smaller type of theatre, called an *odeon*, where concerts, recitals of poetry and musical competitions were held.

Tiles

Builders needed large numbers of tiles. Tiles were made in moulds that were then fired in very large batches in kilns. There were all sorts of different tiles. Perhaps the most common were the roof tiles – flat with ridges (called a *tegula*), with a half-round one (an *imbrex*) to link two flat ones together. There were also large, flat tiles to support the floors above the **hypocaust** heating system, and box tiles to take the hot air up through the walls.

Roman civilization. The historian **Tacitus** writes this about the general Agricola conquering new peoples in **Britain**: 'He educated the sons of the chiefs … the result of this was that instead of loathing the **Latin** language they became keen to speak it properly. In the same way our national dress came into favour and the toga was seen everywhere.'

Towns

See **Cities and new towns**.

This triangular roof tile, an 'antefix', decorated the edge of tiled roofs. It carries the name of the 20th legion (LEG XX) and the legion's mascot, which was a charging boar. The tile was probably made for one of the buildings of the fortress of the legion.

Toga

This type of woollen garment could be worn only by citizens – therefore, men. It is often seen on statues of politicians and **emperors**. The toga was worn mainly for ceremonial and public occasions. Boys whose fathers were citizens wore the *toga praetexta*, which was a toga with a purple border (see **Clothes**).

The toga was considered so important as the dress of a citizen of **Rome** that it became a symbol for

This bronze statuette is of a 'lictor', wearing a toga and carrying the symbols of power of senior magistrates. On his shoulder are the 'fasces', bundles of rods (a symbol of the power to beat people) and an axe (a symbol of the power to execute offenders).

131

Toys and games

'I had a good win playing dice – and I didn't cheat.'
Scribbled on a bath-house in Pompeii

These are dice used for games. The top one has Roman numerals (see **Numbers**) carved into green stone. The one below it on the left is made from rock crystal. The dice on the right is carved from agate.

Some Roman **children** had all sorts of toys to play with and games to enjoy. Miniature **animals**, people, carts and chariots have been found. There were rag dolls and 'squeaky' animals for babies – perhaps a hollow pig with a rattle inside. Marbles, made of **glass** or **pottery**, were also popular.

There were indoor games for children and adults. Some used special boards with dice to throw. A type of dice game was played using the knucklebones of sheep. Scores were kept for the different four sides of the bones that landed upwards. Other dice games that were popular included *Twelve Lines* (a sort of backgammon game), and *Robbers* (which was especially popular with soldiers). In this game, the counters had different values, and players had to capture their opponents' pieces.

There were also lots of outdoor games. Apart from the really energetic

Carved into the passageways that lead to the amphitheatre in Italica are these 'boards', which were used for games employing dice and counters.

ones, such as wrestling, bowling a hoop and ball games were also popular. One ball game, called *trigon*, involved three people standing in a triangle quickly throwing a hard ball to one another. Another was called *harpastum* and this game involved players trying to snatch away a heavy ball.

This child's toy in the shape of a horse was discovered in Egypt.

This complete game, with a board of stone, dice, shakers and bone counters, was found at the military town of Corbridge on Hadrian's Wall in Britain.

The pieces for Roman games: above are knucklebones made from gemstones and glass; on the right are marbles made of multicoloured glass and pottery; while below are carved bone counters from Egypt – look for a hare, the head of a ram and a lobster.

*This Roman child's rag doll, fashioned in Egypt, is made of linen filled with rags and pieces of papyri (see **Writing**).*

133

Trajan

Trajan came from the city of **Italica**, near modern Seville in Spain, and was the first **emperor** who did not come from Italy. He served as a tribune (see **Officials**) under his father and later was a governor in **Germany**. He was adopted as the heir of the emperor Nerva and was declared emperor in AD 98 on Nerva's death. Perhaps his greatest military campaign was against the Dacians. These wars were recorded on **Trajan's Column**, which he had carved and erected in

Rome. He spent his final years on campaign and died after a stroke in Cilicia (a **province** in the eastern part of the **empire**) in AD 117. The emperor's cremated remains were buried in a golden urn at the base of his famous column.

*A gold coin featuring a portrait of the emperor Trajan. His name can clearly be seen on the left after the letters IMP (see **Emperor**).*

A marble bust of the emperor Trajan.

Trajan's Column

The emperor **Trajan** invaded Dacia (modern Romania) in two campaigns (in AD 101 and again in 105) with the intention of conquering that country for **Rome**. The **invasion** was successful and Dacia became a Roman **province** in AD 106. The **emperor** put up a splendid monument to this victory in the form of a spiral column in Rome as part of a large complex of a **forum**, **basilica** and libraries. It stood just over 41 m (135 ft) high and once had a **statue** of Trajan on top. This statue was removed in the medieval period and was later replaced with one of St Peter.

The column itself is made from nineteen huge drums of marble completely covered with the most intricate carving depicting the

Trajan's campaigns in Dacia are recorded in incredible detail on his column. The central portion, to the left of the hole, shows Trajan addressing his troops. Among the group of soldiers are several carrying the standards of their legions.

The other side of Trajan's gold coin (see opposite) has an illustration of his famous column on it. The column is topped with a the statue of the emperor, which is now lost.

campaign in Dacia in a frieze 200 m (656 ft) in length. Amazingly, this frieze includes more than 2,600 figures. Here you can see the whole military life – from marching soldiers to constructing an overnight camp, from soldiers crossing rivers to attacking enemy towns using the *testudo*, from the emperor addressing his troops to the defeated Dacian ambassadors submitting themselves to Trajan. Trajan's Column is an extraordinary piece of evidence for the Roman **army**, its equipment and the workings of the military

When Trajan died he received a final honour – his remains were allowed to be buried inside the limits of the city (see **Burials and tombstones**). He was cremated and his ashes placed in a golden urn that was placed in the base of his great column.

People who lived in Rome, or who visited the city, could see the emperor's extraordinary deeds carved into the column. A coin was also minted to let people throughout the **empire** know about this famous column.

Trier

The people who lived in the north-western part of the Roman **province** of **Gaul** were called the Treveri. The emperor **Augustus** created a new city (see **Cities and new towns**) at Trier in 15–13 BC and called it Augusta Treverorum, which means 'the city of the Treveri people founded by Augustus'. Much later, the emperor **Constantine** lived there and built a **Christian** cathedral, the largest **baths** outside **Rome**, a palace and a great **basilica**.

Triumphs

When a Roman general won a great military victory or campaign, the **senate** could vote him a triumph. This usually involved a great procession, led by magistrates and senators, to **sacrifice** to the **god Jupiter** on the Capitol in **Rome**. Booty taken from the enemy, prisoners of war and paintings or models of battles or cities won by the Roman **army** were displayed. White oxen were led in the procession for sacrifice to Jupiter.

Next came the triumphal general, who might also be the **emperor**, riding in a chariot drawn by four horses. He would be splendidly dressed with a crown of laurel leaves on his head and his face would be painted red. The Romans were a very superstitious people. To ward off the evil eye the general wore an amulet and a **slave** whispered to him, 'Remember you are only a man'.

Behind the general came the army who shouted 'Behold the Triumph!' but they also cheered and shouted coarse expressions or sang bawdy songs. The procession gradually filed through the city, the chief prisoner was executed in the **forum** and the sacrifices took place at the **temple** of **Jupiter** built on the Capitoline Hill.

During the time of the **empire** only an emperor could celebrate a triumph, and

'*Notice was posted of the day the triumphal procession was to take place and, on the day, not a soul of the countless multitudes in Rome stayed at home. They all left their homes and occupied every position they could, only leaving room for the procession which they were to gaze upon.*'
Josephus, on the triumph celebrated by Vespasian and Titus in AD 71 after the Jewish War

This clay relief shows prisoners from Trajan's campaign in Dacia being paraded in a triumphal procession through the city of Rome.

This triumphal arch was dedicated to the emperor Titus by the 'senate and people of Rome' to commemorate his deification (being declared a god) and for his victories over the Jews (see **Masada**).

they often built triumphal arches as a permanent memorial to a famous victory. Triumphal arches that are still standing in Rome today were built to celebrate the victory over Maxentius by the emperor **Constantine**, the taking of Jerusalem by **Vespasian** and Titus, and the Parthian campaigns of Septimius Severus.

Many other triumphal arches still survive in other parts of the former Roman empire – for example, in the provinces of **Gaul**, in **Britain** (in the city of **Colchester**) and in north **Africa**.

Trousers

For the fashionable Roman city dweller, trousers were considered to be the dress of a **barbarian**. But trousers and breeches were worn by many men. Working people, especially on **farms**, wore trousers or strips of cloth wrapped around their legs below their tunics. Soldiers wore breeches that came down to just below the knee (see **Clothes**).

U

Underclothes

The most common form of underclothes for men and **women** in the Roman world was the loincloth, which was called a *subligaculum*. As well as this garment, **women** could also wear briefs and a breastband called a *strophium* (brassiere).

Actual two-piece 'bikinis' have been found in excavations in **London**, and examples pictured on **mosaics** are worn by athletes or dancers.

Socks were a very commonly worn article of underclothing by men and women. There are some examples of ankle socks but most were knee-high.

Above: This pair of leather briefs was made in the 1st century AD. They were found during excavations in London.

This Roman mosaic comes from the baths in a private villa in Sicily and shows two women wearing leather briefs and breastbands that look like bikinis.

Vandals

The people known as the Vandals originally came from central Europe but they swept westwards through Spain (called **Hispania** by the Romans) into north **Africa** early in the 5th century AD.

In the 3rd century AD the emperor Aurelian had trouble with the Vandals. He defeated them in battle in AD 271, at which point the Vandal chieftains asked for a treaty with **Rome**. The chieftains offered their own sons as hostages and in addition the emperor Aurelian demanded that 2,000 of their cavalry should serve in the Roman army. The great horde of Vandals then went home beyond the River Danube – the northern border of the Roman empire. The emperor **Justinian** campaigned successfully against the Vandals in Africa in AD 533 and won back the territory for the eastern Roman **empire**.

Venus

Venus, the mother of **Aeneas**, was originally a goddess (see **Gods and goddesses**) who was worshipped as a spirit of garden fertility. Later she became identified with the **Greek** goddess Aphrodite and so became associated with love and beauty. **Julius Caesar** claimed that he was descended from the goddess Venus. He and the emperor **Hadrian** both built **temples** for her in **Rome**. The month of April, as the beginning of spring, was thought to be sacred to Venus.

The image of a Vandal on horseback, from a mosaic made in around AD 500 in Carthage, north Africa.

Vespasian

Vespasian was unlike all the previous Roman **emperors** because he did not come from a **patrician** family. Instead, his background was middle-class. Before becoming head of state, Vespasian had an honourable public career as tribune, praetor, **consul** and governor in **Africa** (see **Officials**). He commanded the 2nd **legion** Augusta during the conquest of **Britain** in AD 43–47. He was favoured by the emperor **Nero**, although he did incur the emperor's displeasure when he fell asleep during one of Nero's famously long musical performances.

The emperor Nero appointed Vespasian to be governor of the **province** of Judaea to suppress the rebellion of the Jews (a part of this campaign was the **siege** of **Masada**). It was during this war that he was declared emperor by the **army**, who had murdered Vitellius, the last of the three emperors who followed on from Nero – Galba (AD 68–69), Otho (AD 69) and Vitellius (AD 69).

Vespasian's reign, which began in AD 70, was a period of stability for **Rome** and,

The head of the emperor Vespasian from a marble statue from Carthage made at the end of the emperor's life.

unlike many other emperors, Vespasian died of natural causes, in AD 79.

Vesta

Vesta was the goddess (see **Gods and goddesses**) of sacred fire, and she was worshipped both in public **temples** as well as in people's houses as one of the **household gods**. Her place of worship in the city of **Rome** was a round building that contained a 'fire which never was let out'. The goddess was served by special priestesses called Vestal Virgins. These priestesses (see **Priests and priestesses**) were girls chosen between the ages of six and ten to serve Vesta for thirty years.

These are the remains of the circular temple of Vesta, which are found in the main forum in Rome, called the Forum Romanum.

This is an artist's impression of the villa at Lullingstone, in southern Britain. It shows how the villa may have looked around the middle of the 4th century AD.

Villas

Today we often use the word 'villa' to mean a holiday house in the country, near the sea or in the mountains. The Romans used the word in the same way, but it could also mean a simple **farm** or a large country farming estate that employed hundreds of workers.

There were many luxury seaside villas that looked out over the Bay of Naples, close to **Pompeii and Herculaneum**. Rich Romans wanted their holiday houses to be as well designed as their **houses** in the city. The *atrium*, or enclosed courtyard, had various rooms around it. Some were bedrooms and one might be the main living room, called the *tablinum*. There might be more than one

triclinium, or dining room, so that the diners could enjoy the sun at different times of the year.

Country or seaside villas would be decorated with **mosaics** and **wall paintings**, but they might also have gardens or even small parks attached to them. For example, **Hadrian**'s villa at Tivoli, near **Rome**, was really a grand palace (and probably an administrative centre), but it had extensive gardens and elaborate water features.

The writer **Pliny** the Younger owned several farming estates. This is how he described part of his villa, with its own **baths**, right on the coast, only 29 km (18 miles) from Rome: 'The villa is the right size for me and not expensive for me to keep up. First you go into the atrium … from there into D-shaped

'Whenever I'm worn out with worry and want to get some rest, I go to my villa.'
Martial

'Gaius Plinius to his dear friend Gallus. Greetings. You are amazed that I am so fond of my villa at Laurentum. You won't be when you see how charming it is – on a fine stretch of seashore and only seventeen miles from Rome. I can spend the night here after a full day's work in the city.'
Pliny the Younger

Inside the villa at Lullingstone (see page 141). The villa has been excavated and is now protected by a modern building. At the far end are the remains of the villa's private baths. The inset picture is a close-up of the mosaic floor that covered the main living room and, in the foreground, the semi-circular dining room. Diners reclined on benches around the edge of the mosaic (see **Houses**).

colonnades enclosing a small but pleasant courtyard … there is a nice dining room which juts out on to the shore. All around the dining room are folding doors or big windows … from the back you can see the woods and in the distance the hills.'

Virgil

Virgil is considered to be the finest of all the Roman poets and is probably the one best known today. He came from a small town near Mantua and wrote during the time of the emperor **Augustus**. Although he wrote poems about the countryside and agriculture (see **Farms**), his most famous work is the *Aeneid*, a twelve-book poem about the epic journey and adventures of the hero **Aeneas**, as he travelled from Troy to Italy.

Vitruvius

Vitruvius was an architect and military engineer who worked on the rebuilding of **Rome** under the emperor **Augustus**. He wrote *About Architecture*, a book full of useful and fascinating information about the planning of towns (see **Cities and new towns**) and the building of **aqueducts**, artillery machines and devices for telling the time.

Voting

Voting in elections was only for citizens, who could only be men. People were assembled together in units for voting.

Vulcan

This lame god of fire and furnaces was worshipped by blacksmiths. Vulcan is often pictured on stone carvings with the blacksmith's tools of a hammer, tongs and anvil (see **Gods and Goddesses**).

'The mat makers ask you to elect Lollius as aedile'

'All the fishermen say, "Elect Popidius Rufus as aedile"'

Slogans painted on the walls of Pompeii

Wall painting

The Romans liked the walls, floors and ceilings of their **houses** to be bright and colourful. A house owner could choose from a number of different subjects and styles, and fashion in interior decoration changed from time to time, just as it does today. Wall painters and **mosaic**-makers carried illustrated catalogues for their customers to choose from. Series of scenes were very popular for large rooms (reception and main living rooms). Subjects included traditional stories about **gods and goddesses** or heroes or large landscape scenes. Most wall paintings were large panels with architectural features (such as columns) between. Some panels, however, were very small – much like paintings hung on a wall – perhaps a still-life of a bowl of fruit with a wine glass, for example.

Because many Roman wall paintings have survived, especially at **Pompeii and Herculaneum**, and because we have **Vitruvius**'s manual for builders and architects, we know quite a lot about the techniques of the wall painter. Vitruvius tells us that several layers of plaster had to be applied to the walls to make a hard, smooth surface. The paint was applied before the last coat was dry so that the paint would soak into the walls and become permanent. This technique is known as *fresco* painting.

There were lots of colours to choose from, mixed from a range of pigments and other materials – for example, black from carbon or soot, white from chalk, red and yellow from ochre, blue from a glass-and-copper mixture and purple from certain types of sea shell.

'When the plastered walls are made solid and have been polished like marble they will look splendid after the colours have been put on. When the colours are carefully put on to wet plaster they do not fade but become permanent.'
Vitruvius

One of the favourite subjects for wall paintings in Roman houses was a landscape scene, often with villas and temples, as here from a house in Pompeii.

143

Above: This is one of the public fountains and water troughs on a street corner in the city of Herculaneum. On the right you can see in detail where the water originally came out. The face is probably that of a water god.

Water supply

The lifestyle of the Romans meant that they needed, and indeed used, very large quantities of water. The average Roman town dweller, for example, used approximately 236 litres (52 gallons) of water each day, which is much more than we use today. The main reason for these vast quantities was simple – there were few taps to turn the water off. Therefore it flowed constantly into **lavatories**, **baths**, water troughs, and so on.

Wells provided some of the supply for the Romans, but most had to be brought into towns and cities by **aqueducts**. The water came through channels and pipes into a reservoir called a *castellum aquae*. In **Pompeii** the reservoir supplied water to lead tanks built on towers constructed throughout the town. Lead pipes then took most of the water

to public fountains, as most people did not have, or were not allowed to have, their own private water supply.

The town appointed an **official** to look after the local water supply. He was called the *curator aquarum*. His team of engineers and labourers had to clean the system, repair the channels, tanks and pipes and stop people from attaching pipes to the public channels for their own use.

Frontinus was a water inspector in **Rome** and in his book called *The Water Supply of Rome* he wrote the following in AD 97: 'The inspector must make sure that no one draws more water from the public system than he has permission for from the **emperor**. He must be on his guard all the time against the many forms of fraud.'

Frontinus estimated that he could provide 1,000 million litres (about 220 million gallons) of water each day for use by the people of Rome.

144

Weapons and armour

Infantry and **cavalry** soldiers used different types of armour and weapons. The legionary soldier (see **Legions and legionaries**) wore a tunic under his armour, strong leather sandals (called *caliga*) with hob nails on the sole to cope with hard use and muddy conditions and to make them last longer, and kept warm by wrapping himself in a large, woollen cloak. His armour (from the 1st century AD) was made from strips of metal joined with straps and buckles.

We also know from evidence found in different excavations that some soldiers wore chain-linked body armour. This protected the top part of his body only. On his head the legionary soldier wore an iron helmet with a neck guard and hinged flaps to cover and protect his cheeks. The legionary soldier was also protected by the rectangular

These armour fittings, made of bronze, held together iron strips that protected the upper part of a soldier's body. You can see hinges (at the top) and buckles where the fittings were attached to leather straps. They were all found at a fort built in Roman Britain.

Made around AD 100, this decorated bronze cavalry helmet comes from northern Britain. It was probably used for sporting competitions and parades rather than battles.

shield (called a *scutum*) he carried. The shield was made of strips of woods glued together and covered with leather or felt. Attached in the centre was a metal boss, or stud, with a handle at the back. The shield weighed about 6 kg (13 lb).

The legionary soldier carried a number of weapons: he would have had a javelin (the *pilum*), which had a wooden shaft with a long metal tip; he fought hand-to-hand using a short dagger (the *pugio*), about 25 cm (10 in) long, and a short sword (the *gladius*), which was about 40–50 cm (16–20 in) in length. The dagger and sword were carried in scabbards hung from two belts with a small apron of metal discs riveted to leather straps.

The cavalryman had a different array of protective clothing and weaponry. He wore body armour, which was short to allow for as much movement as possible in the saddle. This armour was usually mail, made from iron rings or small scales of metal laced together with leather thongs. Like the infantry soldier, he wore an iron helmet and carried a shield, but his was oval in shape. He also carried spears or javelins.

Some cavalry troops were equipped with bows and arrows or sling shots. The cavalryman also carried a long sword (called a *spatha*), which was 65–80 cm (25–31 in) long and was carried on his right side.

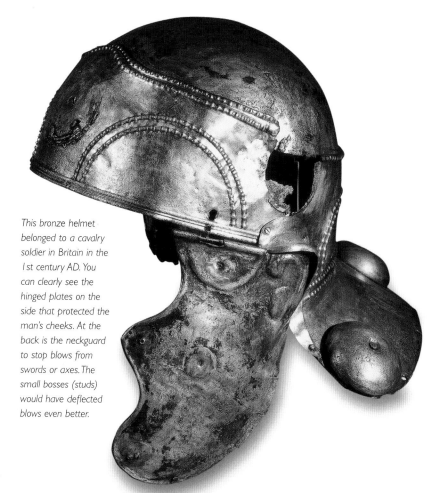

This bronze helmet belonged to a cavalry soldier in Britain in the 1st century AD. You can clearly see the hinged plates on the side that protected the man's cheeks. At the back is the neckguard to stop blows from swords or axes. The small bosses (studs) would have deflected blows even better.

*Below: The helmet and shield of a legionary soldier, both made of bronze. The helmet has a neckguard (on the right). LEG VIII and a picture of a bull, the legion's symbol, tell us that the shield belonged to a soldier serving in the 8th legion, which was stationed in northern Britain in the early 2nd century AD. We even know the owner's name because of the inscription IVL MAGNI IVNI DVBITATI, which means 'the property of Dubitatus of Julius Magnus's century'. A century was a unit in a legion (see **Army**).*

*Right: Legionaries used an iron stabbing sword (gladius) like this. It was found in London and dates from the 1st century AD. It has lost its handle (probably wood) and the leather parts of its sheath, on the far right. Look closely at the sheath and you will see a wolf and two children (see **Romulus and Remus**).*

Above: These weapons were all found at a Roman fort in Britain. On the left are two javelins and next to them is a dagger with its sheath.

147

A wedding ceremony with the couple holding hands is pictured on this marble relief carving from Rome. The bridegroom is holding the written contract for the marriage in his left hand.

Weddings

Roman marriages were often arranged between **families**, and couples were married at an early age. There would be an engagement ceremony, a *sponsalia*, when the girl was usually about twelve and the boy fourteen. But it was not unusual for a teenage girl to be engaged to a man much older than herself. He might even have been married more than once before. At the *sponsalia* the future husband would give the girl gifts, including a ring. A contract would be signed and the ceremony sealed with a kiss.

It was important to choose the right wedding day. The second half of June was considered the luckiest. There were different marriage ceremonies but the most popular was held at the home of the girl. The ceremony was called the *confarreatio*. The bride wore a pure white tunic and a flame-coloured veil over her head. On her feet were flame-coloured sandals. After **sacrificing** (usually) a pig, the innards were inspected for omens or signs and the girl said, U*bi tu Gaius, ego Gaia* ('Whichever family you belong to, I also belong'). All the guests shouted F*eliciter* ('Good Luck') and the marriage was sealed by the couple holding hands.

The guests carried traditional sweets and sesame cakes, and nuts were thrown to the children for luck. The husband then led his wife to their new home and carried her over the threshold. The husband had to be very careful because stumbling was thought to bring very bad luck.

Weights and measures

There were offices in Roman towns for inspectors of weights and measures. They went to **shops** and workshops to check that people were paying for the right quantities. Here are some weights and measure and their modern equivalents:

Libra – the Roman pound weight (equivalent to 327.45 g), which was divided into 12 *unciae* (ounces).
Sextarius – mainly used as a measure for liquid but also used for measuring grain (equivalent to 454 ml or 0.96 pint).
Amphora – this was not only a type of storage jar, but also a measure of volume (equivalent to 25.79 litres or 5.67 gallons).
Pes – the Roman foot measured 29.46 cm (11½ in) divided into 12 *unciae*.
Mille passuum – the Roman mile (1,475 m), which is just short of an English mile.
Actus quadratus – a measure of a square area of 120 Roman feet.

Wine

Vineyards were common throughout the Roman world. Grapes were pressed into juice and the better quality wine was put into huge storage jars, called **amphorae**, and shipped to city **shops** and restaurants. **Ships** carried huge numbers of amphorae containing wine. One was calculated to hold 6,000 amphorae, which would amount to 144,000 litres (32,000 gallons). Wine could be drunk as it was but was nearly always watered down. Sometimes other ingredients were added.

Market inspectors used this official equipment to check on the correct measurement of liquids being sold at the town of Dion, in northern Greece.

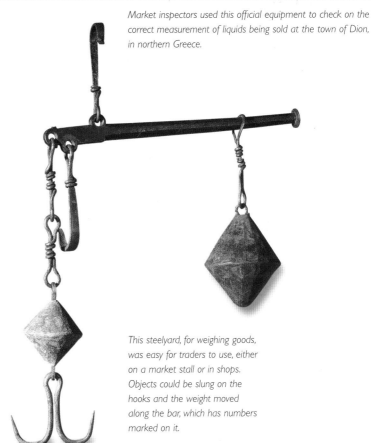

This steelyard, for weighing goods, was easy for traders to use, either on a market stall or in shops. Objects could be slung on the hooks and the weight moved along the bar, which has numbers marked on it.

A popular drink in Roman bars was called *conditum*, which was wine with hot water, honey, pepper and spices added (see **Eating out**). Wine was also reduced by boiling to form a sweet drink or an ingredient in cooking – called *defrutum*. Wine that had gone flat, or bad, was made into vinegar for flavouring sauces. Very watered-down wine made a refreshing drink for marching soldiers.

'Get everything ready that is needed for making the wine. Wash out the vats and repair the baskets. Gather the not-so-good grapes for the coarse wine for the workers to drink.'
Cato

Women

The position of most women in Roman society was almost exclusively in the home. While it was usual for a man to pursue a career or run a business, women were generally expected to bear **children** and run the household. When a man died, male guardians would be appointed to look after his sons, daughters and wife. Far fewer girls than boys went to **school** and women were not allowed to vote in elections.

Some women, however, ran their own businesses, in particular **shops**, and had occupations such as midwives, hairdressers and dressmakers. Wealthy women might have a great deal of independence or even influence. At the other end of the scale, large numbers of women worked as **slaves** (some even as **gladiators**) and many free-born women worked in **houses**, workshops, shops or on **farms**.

Below: A variety of writing materials. On the left are wooden tablets that once held wax; on the right are inkpots and pens.

Above: Bone hairpins were often decorated with heads or objects. This one shows a woman with an elaborate hairstyle.

Writing

Fragments of Roman writing can be seen in many museums today. They are usually in the form of inscriptions carved on stone or words scratched on pieces of **pottery** or **tiles**. For example, a tile worker in Roman **London** scratched these words about his workmate: 'Austalis has been skiving off by himself every day for the last thirteen days!'

Below: An inscription from the triumphal arch of emperor Claudius in Rome. You can see the first few letters of his name at the top. The inscription records Claudius's victorious campaign in Britain.

'To Sulpicia Lepidina, wife of Cerialis, from Severa.

Claudia Severa to her Lepidina greetings. On 11 September, sister, for the day of the celebration of my birthday, I give you a warm invitation to make sure that you come to us, to make the day more enjoyable for me by your arrival, if you are present. Give my greetings to your Cerialis. My Aelius and my little son send him their greetings. I shall expect you sister. Farewell, sister my dearest soul, as I hope to prosper, and hail.'

Above: The birthday invitation translated here is one of the earliest known examples of handwriting in Latin by a woman. The note was sent by Claudia Severa to her friend, the commander's wife,

Sulpicia Lepidina. It was written, between AD 97 and 103, probably by a professional secretary and only the last two sentences were written by Severa herself.

'... I have sent you ... pairs of socks from Sattua, two pairs of sandals and two pairs of underpants ...'
Fragments of a letter to a soldier stationed at the fort of Vindolanda near Hadrian's Wall

The Romans had not discovered paper but they wrote on four different types of material. The most expensive and finest writing material was vellum. It is made from very thin sheets of animal skin (usually young goat or lamb) and it was used for scrolls. Papyrus comes from the leaves of a plant that grows near rivers, especially in **Egypt**. Pens and ink were used to write on papyrus, which would be used for recording legal documents, for example. The Romans did not use books, as we know them, until the 4th century AD and the papyrus was made in scrolls.

The third type of writing material was wax tablets. These were small and very shallow wooden boxes into which melted wax was poured, and they were written on using a *stylus*. This instrument was pointed at one end, to scratch the letters, and flat at the other end, to smooth off the wax so it could be used again. Wax tablets were used for writing notes, sending messages or packing lists or for making shopping lists.

Finally, very thin shavings of wood were used for writing on. These were the cheapest form of writing material and could be folded into small sheets and tied together into bundles. Some of these have been found preserved in the excavations of the Roman **fort** of Vindolanda, south of **Hadrian's Wall** in **Britain**. They were used to keep lists of goods and supplies and to send letters to and from soldiers.

Y

York

York, called Eboracum by the Romans, was one of the places **legions** were stationed in a large **fort** during the **invasion** and occupation of **Britain**. Eboracum was the home of the 9th legion.

From the end of the 1st century AD, York was the military capital of Britain. As in so many other places in the **provinces**, a **settlement** grew up outside the fort and eventually a new town was established (see **Cities and new towns**). York became one of the most important

An artist's impression of building work on the walls of York in the 3rd century AD.

towns in Roman Britain and, during the 4th century AD, it was one of the two northern capitals of the reorganized province of Britain.

York was associated with several **emperors**. The emperor Severus died in York in AD 211 and Constantius I carried out work on the defences after the barbarian destruction in AD 296. His son, **Constantine the Great**, was proclaimed emperor in the city in AD 306.

The end of the Roman period in Britain was not the end of the city of York. We know that it was occupied by the Anglo-Saxons – Edwin the King of Northumbria was baptised a Christian there in AD 627. Later it became the capital of the Viking kingdom and the new occupiers called it Jorvik.

Zama

One of **Rome**'s most difficult enemies to overcome was the Carthaginian general, **Hannibal**. The Roman commander, Publius Cornelius Scipio, had defeated the Carthaginian armies in Spain between 210 and 206 BC. He then pursued Hannibal to north **Africa**.

The most important battle that was fought between the two countries was at Zama, in the autumn of 202 BC. The Romans under Scipio had 23,000 infantry soldiers and 6,000 **cavalry** (see **Legions and legionaries**). In Hannibal's **army** there were 36,000 infantry and 4,000 cavalry. This Carthaginian army, which was arranged in long blocks, also had some war elephants. Scipio sent his light-armed troops against the elephants, leaving spaces between small units of troops to let them escape through to the rear. Meanwhile the Roman cavalry came around to attack from the sides and then came back to attack the great Carthaginian army from the rear. The Carthaginians were massacred while the Romans lost very few troops.

This is the tombstone of a woman called Julia Velva, who died aged fifty and was buried in York. The scene shows the feast at Julia's funeral. She reclines on a couch while food is laid out on a little three-legged table. We know from the inscription that the man standing on the right is called Aurelius Mercurialis and that she has left him her property. Perhaps he is her son-in-law, the girl sitting on the left her daughter and the little boy between them her grandson.

After this huge defeat the Carthaginians had to agree peace terms with the Romans. Hannibal pulled out of Spain, and had to pay a large fine and give rewards to the African allies of the Romans, the Numidians. Because of his military success against Hannibal in Africa, Scipio was given the honour of adding the name Africanus to his own.

Zenobia

Zenobia's husband, Odaenath, was king of **Palmyra**. After his murder in AD 266, Zenobia became queen. Although an ally of Rome, she invaded **Egypt** and also occupied a large area of the Roman **province** of **Asia**.

At first the Roman **emperor** Aurelian did nothing about her revolt, but when she had her son, Vaballath, proclaimed emperor, Aurelian marched east and fought her. He captured Palmyra and she was taken prisoner. Zenobia was taken to **Rome** and exhibited in a triumphal procession (see **Triumphs**) in AD 272. She was given a pension, a **villa** just outside Rome and lived there until her old age.

Z

The Roman emperors

Augustus

Hadrian

	180–192 Commodus	**211** Geta	**222–235** Alexander Severus	**Gallic empire**
				260–269 Postumus
	193 Pertinax	**211–217** Caracalla	**235–238** Maximinus Thrax	**269** Laelianus
	193 Didius Julianus	**217–218** Macrinus	**238** Gordian I and	**269** Marius
	193–211 Septimius Severus	**218–222** Elagabalus	Gordian II (in Africa)	**268–271** Victorinus
27 BC–AD 14 Augustus	**79–81** Titus		**238** Balbinus and Pupienus (in Italy)	**268–271** Victorinus
14–37 Tiberius	**81–96** Domitian		**238–244** Gordian III	**271–274** Tetricus
37–41 Caligula	**96–98** Nerva		**244–249** Philip	**268–270** Claudius II
41–54 Claudius	**98–117** Trajan		**249–251** Decius	**270** Quintillus
54–68 Nero	**117–138** Hadrian		**251–253** Trebonianus Gallus	**270–275** Aurelian
68–69 Galba	**138–161** Antoninus Pius		**253** Aemilianus	**275–276** Tacitus
69 Otho	**161–180** Marcus Aurelius (161–169 with Lucius Verus)		**253–260** Valerian	**276** Florianus
69 Vitellius				**276–282** Probus
69–79 Vespasian			**253–268** Gallienus	**282–283** Carus

Constantine the Great

		East	West	
		364–378 Valens	**364–375** Valentinian I	**472** Olybrius
283–284 Numerian	**307–337** Constantine I (the Great)	**379–395** Theodosius I	**367–383** Gratian	**473–474** Glycerius
		395–408 Arcadius	**375–392** Valentinian II	**474–475** Nepos
283–285 Carinus		**408–450** Theodosius II	**392–394** Eugenius	**465–476** Romulus Augustulus
284–305 Diocletian	**308–324** Licinius	**450–457** Marcian	**395–423** Honorius	**Barbarian rulers of Italy**
287–305 Maximian	**337–350** Constans	**457–474** Leo	**423–425** Iohannes	**476–493** Odoacer
305–306 Constantius I	**337–361** Constantius II	**474–491** Zeno	**425–455** Valentinian III	**493–526** Theoderic
305–311 Galerius	**360–363** Julian	**491–518** Anastasius	**455** Petronius Maximus	**526–534** Athalaric
306–307 Severus II	**363–364** Jovian	**518–527** Justin	**455–456** Avitus	**534–536** Theodahad
306–312 Maxentius		**527–565** Justinian	**457–461** Majorian	
310–313 Maximinus Daia			**461–465** Severus III	
			467–472 Anthemius	

Justinian

155

Index

Bold page numbers = main entries

Acknowledgements

Pictures are © The British Museum, photographs taken by the British Museum Photographic Service, with the exception of those listed below.

Map artwork by Stefan Chabluk. Trail icons by David Bootle.

Thanks to Mike Charles and Roger White for the use of their photographs.

p. 9: The J. Paul Getty Museum
pp. 10–11 all: Mike Corbishley
p. 13: Mike Corbishley
p. 14 top left: S. Grandadam/Robert Harding; bottom right: The J. Paul Getty Museum
p. 15 both: Mike Corbishley
p. 16 bottom: Mike Corbishley
p. 17: M. Jenner/Robert Harding
p. 18 top left: Mike Corbishley
p. 20 top right: Gloucester City Museum and Art Gallery; bottom left: Mike Corbishley
p. 21: English Heritage Photographic Library
p. 24 bottom: Mike Corbishley
p. 28 top and bottom left: English Heritage Photographic Library; bottom right: Peter Clayton
p. 29: Peter Clayton
p. 30 bottom: Peter Clayton
p. 32 top: Colchester Museums
p. 37: Sonia Halliday Photographs
p. 39: The J. Paul Getty Museum, gift of Barbara and Lawrence Fleischman
pp. 40–41: Colchester Archaeological Trust © Peter Froste
p. 41: Colchester Archaeological Trust
pp. 42–43: Mike Corbishley
p. 43: Mike Corbishley
pp. 44–45: Mike Corbishley
p. 45: Peter Clayton
p. 47: English Heritage Photographic Library
p. 48 right: Ronald Sheridan at Ancient Art & Architecture Collection
p. 52 bottom: Mike Corbishley
p. 54: Sonia Halliday/photograph by F.H.C. Birch
p. 56: National Museums of Scotland
p. 60 top: Mike Corbishley; bottom: English Heritage Photographic Library
p. 61 top: Mike Corbishley; bottom: English Heritage Photographic Library
p. 62 bottom: Mike Corbishley
p. 67: Mike Corbishley
p. 69 top left: Mike Corbishley; bottom: English Heritage Photographic Library
p. 70: The J. Paul Getty Museum
p. 71 bottom right: Peter Clayton
p. 72: Mike Corbishley
p. 73 bottom: Mike Corbishley
p. 75: Mike Charles
p. 76: Mike Corbishley
p. 77: Mike Corbishley

p. 79 left: The J. Paul Getty Museum
p. 81: The J. Paul Getty Museum
p. 83 bottom both: English Heritage Photographic Library
p. 84 bottom: Sonia Halliday/photograph by Valerie Williams
p. 85 top: English Heritage Photographic Library; inset: Mike Corbishley
p. 87: Museum of London
p. 91: Sonia Halliday Photographs
p. 93 left: The J. Paul Getty Museum
p. 95 left: Mike Corbishley
p. 100 left: The J. Paul Getty Museum
p. 101: Peter Clayton
pp. 102–103 all: Mike Corbishley
p. 104: P. Hawkins/Robert Harding
p. 106: Photo SCALA, Florence
p. 107: Mike Corbishley
p. 108 top and bottom left: Lesley & Roy Adkins Picture Library; inset: Mike Corbishley
p. 109: Mike Corbishley
p. 110 both: Lesley & Roy Adkins Picture Library
p. 111 top left and right: Lesley & Roy Adkins Picture Library
p. 114 bottom right: Mike Corbishley
p. 115 bottom left: Mike Corbishley
pp. 116–117: Mike Corbishley
p. 117 bottom: Photo SCALA, Florence
p. 119: The J. Paul Getty Museum
p. 120: Mike Corbishley
p. 121 inset: Mike Corbishley
p. 122 bottom both: Mike Corbishley
p. 123: Mike Corbishley
p. 124 both: Mike Corbishley
p. 125 bottom: The Bridgeman Art Library
p. 126: The J. Paul Getty Museum
p. 127 top left and inset: Mike Corbishley
p. 128: Mike Corbishley
p. 129 top: Peter Clayton; bottom: Mike Corbishley
p. 130: Mike Corbishley
p. 132 top right: Mike Corbishley
p. 133 top left: English Heritage Photographic Library
p. 135 top: Mike Corbishley
p.137: Mike Corbishley
p. 138 inset: Museum of London; right: Sonia Halliday Photographs
p. 139: Michael Holford
p. 140 bottom: Peter Clayton
p. 141: English Heritage Photographic Library
p. 142 both: Mike Corbishley
p. 143: Lesley & Roy Adkins Picture Library
p. 144 both: Mike Corbishley
p. 149 top: Mike Corbishley
p. 150 middle: Roger White
p. 152: English Heritage Photographic Library
p. 153: York Museums Trust (Yorkshire Museum)